O F
POETRY
A N D
POWER

OF POETRY

POEMS OCCASIONED

AND BY THE DEATH

Foreword by Arthur Schlesinger, Jr.

AND POWER

BY THE PRESIDENCY
OF JOHN F. KENNEDY

EDITED WITH AN INTRODUCTION

by Erwin A. Glikes and Paul Schwaber

BASIC BOOKS, INC.

PUBLISHERS / NEW YORK

FOREWORD

There is a sad felicity in the fact that the murder of John Fitz-gerald Kennedy should have provoked this memorial volume. This is in part because poetry had a prominent place in President Kennedy's own vision of America. He saw his country as not just a political establishment or an economic system or a web of legal relationships. All these were for him aspects of a larger conception—America as a civilized society. He believed that the arts were the source and sign of a serious civilization, and one of his constant concerns while in the White House was to accord artists a nation's belated recognition of their vital role. He considered the arts essential, not only for their own sake, but for the health of the state; for, among other things, art could provide a necessary check on and criticism of authority. His sense of the relationship between poetry and power was not casual or whimsical. It was organic and profound.

But his recognition of the place of the artist is, I think, the lesser reason for the appropriateness of this volume. The greater reason lies in the fact that President Kennedy himself shared so much of the vision of life which has animated the greatest poetry. He once described himself as an "idealist without illu-sions." He understood both the potentialities of humanity and the precariousness of the human condition. He admired Robert Frost, for example, not as a good gray rustic philosopher, but as an artist who confronted the somber cruelties of experience without fuss or sentimentality. From without, Kennedy's life sometimes seemed easy and privileged; but this was so in only a limited sense. His brother has told us: "At least one-half of the days that he spent on this earth were days of intense physi-cal pain." He brushed extremely close to death several times before the terrible day in Dallas. He lived, moreover, in an age which had been an ordeal of historical disillusion, leaving so few things on which mature man could rely—family, friendship, physical courage, intellectual discipline, wit, reason, power. With

Foreword

such a life and in such a world, he chose to distance himself
from displays of emotion.

In consequence, some thought him detached or indifferent.
But only the unwary could really conclude that his "coolness"
was because he felt too little. It was because he felt too much
and had to compose himself for an existence filled with disorder
and suffering. At a press conference, he once remarked about
the demobilization of the reserves after the Berlin crisis: "There
is always an inequity in life. Some men are killed in a war and
some men are wounded, and some men never leave the country.
. . . Life is unfair." He said this, not with bitterness, but with
the delicate knowledge of one who lives in a bitter time—a
knowledge which stamped him as a son of that time. Some
poems in this collection evoke his charm and grace, occasionally
almost with envy. But the Kennedy style was not an uncove-
nanted gift. It was the triumph, hard-bought and well-earned, of
a gallant and collected human being over the anguish of life.

A number of poems describe in various ways the fragility of our
civilization, "the brute in us," the monsters of violence lurking
beneath the façades of order. Kennedy himself was desperately
aware of what one poem calls "the thin fabric of law between
reason and chaos." This awareness committed him to the un-
ceasing fight to preserve and reinforce that fabric, whether
against nuclear war or against unendurable social injustice. He
knew that he always must keep his country and his world moving fast enough to prevent violence from rending the membrane
of civility. Supremely a man of reason, he understood the depths
of unreason in human nature and sought within the time he
had to strengthen the decencies of life against the demons of
destruction.

These things, much more than his royal role as patron of the
arts, account, I think, for these poems. So many of the writers
identify themselves with him—"I too am dead"; "We all were
passengers in that motorcade"; "I am the vain one,/ a bullet in
my shoulder, six seconds to go/ before another burns in my
head"—and they do so because they perceived in him, not just
another American president, but *mon semblable, mon frère*, who,

as much as the poets themselves, felt the terror of the age and, in striving to master both terror and himself, challenged the self-pitying notion so cherished in our nuclear epoch of the abjectness of the individual in the face of history. The editors note that for some he closed the gap between public and private experience. This surely was so, and it was surely because he held out hope that the humane purposes of private man might still influence the unfolding of public events, that mankind was not necessarily impotent before the awful forces man himself had set in motion, that man could be not only victim but hero. "If we filled the day with bravery," said Emerson of the Poet, "we should not shrink from celebrating it."

"Each substance of a grief," wrote Shakespeare, "hath twenty shadows." What the poets here call the "sound of torn strings," the "tumult of images," reveals the variety of ways in which the life and death of Kennedy pierced the sensibilities of his contemporaries. Together the poems convey the impact an emphatic man can have on his times, even in this age of nuclear missiles and the exploration of space—an impact which death will not end, for death cannot invade that region of possibility where, in the words of one poet,

> There, still, your bright incontinent essence
> Inclines to its own completion, still
> Shapes almost its own actuality, still contrives
> Some reason, measure, humor in our lives.

ARTHUR SCHLESINGER, JR.

CONTENTS

O F
POETRY
A N D
POWER

INTRODUCTION

Three months after the assassination of Abraham Lincoln, a large memorial anthology composed primarily of newspaper verse was compiled. None of the now-famous Lincoln elegies found their way into that book. A poem by William Cullen Bryant did appear, but so did poems by "Mrs. F. W. Hall, 70 years of age," and " 'May' of Sparrow Bush, 13 years of age." The best anthology of poems about Lincoln—which included Melville's "The Martyr," Lowell's "Ode Recited at the Harvard Commemoration," and Whitman's "When Lilacs Last in the Dooryard Bloom'd"—was not published until thirty years after Lincoln's death. And yet, all three of these enduring poems were actually written in 1865, the year of the assassination.

Immediately after the assassination of John F. Kennedy, poems began to be written about it and the man it had taken. *The New York Times,* the *Saturday Review,* and even the London *Times Literary Supplement* were inundated with them. For the most part, these poems were more notable for their sincerity than for their quality. It was after seeing a few clearly excellent poems that appeared in December, 1963, that we thought of writing to poets of recognized accomplishment to ask whether they had, in the immediate aftermath of the tragedy, written anything which might be appropriate for such a volume as this. Some of these poets were known only to other poets; others were of national and international reputation. In our letters, we promised to publish a book only if the response indicated that our assumption was correct—that a large body of fine poetry on this subject did, in fact, exist. We wanted the poems to be available to the generation that had lived with John F. Kennedy and must now live with the fact of his death.

The response to our inquiries was overwhelming. Kathleen Raine, for example, wrote from England:

> I am glad to have an opportunity given me by your letter of expressing, if not publicly, at least not quite privately, the profound

Introduction

sorrow I felt at the death of President Kennedy. It was like a personal bereavement, the loss of one of the family made up of one's dear friends. I am as a rule utterly unmoved by public events, and cynical about politicians, but this was altogether different. I mourned when France fell to the Germans, but not again over anything in that way until the death of Kennedy. I had been in Washington during that flowering of poetry, music and all the arts that made his presidency seem like a renaissance (or naissance) and was present at the dinner given for Robert Frost's 88th birthday. Now Frost is gone, and John Kennedy, and Pope John XXIII; and one realizes that even now great men, and above all good men, can change the world of masses and anonymity. But what a year of bereavements—. Only, of course, death immortalizes. One never associated Kennedy with tragedy, with his youth and idealism and the joyfulness of his moment. He raised the United States to a great height; and I feel, as many do, that the grandeur of the national mourning was upon that level to which he had tried to raise his nation; even in spite of the fearful depths the assassination revealed. But they are always there, the heights perhaps not. . . .

Miss Raine's letter eloquently stated feelings expressed in much of the mail received. Most correspondents acknowledged the appropriateness of such a book, and many immediately sent poems that they had written shortly after the assassination.

Some, however, were skeptical. They argued that the uses of poetry had changed irrevocably since Lincoln's day; its matter and manner had become far more private; it no longer assumed a wide audience; nor could it properly attempt a public voice and a public responsibility. Therefore, the prospects of such a book succeeding as a collection of contemporary poetry rather than as a curious document of historical interest seemed to them slight.

The number of good poems we received week after week, however, made us feel that these widely held views of the nature and uses of contemporary poetry ought to be re-examined. There certainly have been changes in poetic styles during the past hundred years, but can they be so easily equated with a complete change in the uses of poetry? After all, if traditional elegiac forms are no longer available, elegiac feeling and ex-

2

pression still are. If admiration and love, grief and fear, are still felt, they can be expressed in poetry and are—though not, of course, as they were in previous ages. If poetry is now more persistently personal in its techniques and concerns than it once was, it nonetheless still reveals and informs human experience. The issue, then, is not whether such feelings can be expressed in modern poetry, but whether a public figure and a public event can inspire them. The answer, we think, is that this president and this event did.

Why this was so is worth pondering. John F. Kennedy's youth, energy, and grace; his intelligence, wit, and evident pleasure in using words skillfully; his political shrewdness that did not depend on cant; his rare ability to revere his office without being solemn about himself—all, doubtless, served to distinguish him for the poets. Miss Raine's letter, for example, speaks of grieving as though for a close friend. Mr. Kennedy's ability to be a successful political figure and at the same time a credible and attractive human being closed, for some, at least, the gap which has developed between public and private experience.

And then, too, there was the event of the assassination itself. It was more than a matter of merely historic and journalistic significance. As it unfolded, an almost-forgotten range of human emotions, from the basest to the most noble, was revealed. As those unforgettable days of late November, 1963, drew relentlessly on, it became clear that we had all witnessed one of the dark, random gestures by which chaos reasserts itself in the universe, tearing through the bright patterns we weave about ourselves and call our civilization. Youth, beauty, noble aspiration (those words revived because he lived) were struck down before our eyes. It was, most properly, a matter for art, for art has met with it before—and will again.

It is, in a way, a tragic irony that so many poems came to be written about John F. Kennedy, for no recent president had been so perceptive of the living role of the poet in the nation's life. Speaking at the dedication of the Robert Frost Library at

Amherst College in October, 1963, President Kennedy praised Frost because

> He brought an unsparing instinct for reality to bear on the platitudes and pieties of society. His sense of the human tragedy fortified him against self-deception and easy consolation.
> "I have been," he wrote, "one acquainted with the night."
> And because he knew the midnight as well as the high noon, because he understood the ordeal as well as the triumph of the human spirit, he gave his age strength with which to overcome despair.

No president had been so gracefully aware of popular American misconceptions about poetry. In a televised interview, President Kennedy once remarked:

> There is a story that some years ago an interested mother wrote to a principal of a school: "Don't teach my boy poetry; he's going to run for Congress." I've never taken the view that the world of politics and the world of poetry are so far apart. I think politicians and poets share at least one thing, and that is that their greatness depends upon the courage with which they face the challenges of life.

Furthermore, no president had so signally honored poetry by asking a poet to participate in the Inauguration, and with such good reasons:

> I asked Robert Frost to come and speak at the Inauguration not merely because I was desirous of according a recognition to his trade, but also because I felt that he had something important to say to those of us who were occupied with the business of government; that he would remind us that we were dealing with life, the hopes and fears of millions of people, and also tell us that our own deep convictions must be the ultimate guide of all our actions.

This was a theme that President Kennedy took up again in his speech at Amherst, which appears as the Appendix to this volume. It is a speech which deserves to be remembered for its statement of the President's faith in "poetry as the means of saving power from itself."

> When power leads man toward arrogance, poetry reminds him of his limitations. When power narrows the areas of man's con-

4

cern, poetry reminds him of the richness and diversity of his existence. When power corrupts, poetry cleanses.

For art establishes the basic human truths which must serve as
the touchstones of our judgment. The artist, however faithful to
his personal vision of reality, becomes the last champion of the
individual mind and sensibility against an intrusive society and an
officious state.

To discover these words among the papers of a deceased head of
state is to realize, again, all we have lost.

The poems that appear in this volume are the work of American and British poets. The poems vary immensely in subject,
approach, and tone; they have in common only their literary accomplishment. The first seven were written during Mr. Kennedy's presidency. Of these, some praise him, and one is sharply
critical. The seventh was written the day before the assassination.
All the other poems were occasioned by the President's sudden
death. There are poems that express shock, anger, horror, and
grief; and there are poems of eulogy and commemoration. A few
explore the psyche of the killer; others, the moral life of the nation. Several are about the limitations of poetry itself attempting to deal with John F. Kennedy's unalterable death.

Certain images and themes recur: President Kennedy's and
Robert Frost's mutual admiration; the Dallas motorcade in the
telescopic sight; the military funeral and the eternal flame; and
Mrs. Kennedy's incredible courage and dignity. Much is made
of the Wild West (distrusted in many of these poems) and of
such symbols of America in the 1960's as supermarkets, heli-
copters, and, of course, television. There are echoes of Whitman's elegy and evocations of a traditional image of evil in
American writing, the spider. Reference is made to classical
patterns and to figures of Shakespearean tragedy. Repeatedly,
poets chose for their titles "November 22, 1963"—a date now
frozen into American history.

The title, *Of Poetry and Power*, is from the penultimate line
of the first poem in this book. In it, Robert Frost heralded

Introduction

John F. Kennedy's inauguration as "the beginning hour" of "A golden age of poetry and power."

Though not composed exclusively of tributes to the late President, this book pays tribute to him. It does so, we believe, in the honesty, variety, and achievement of the individual poems it contains. President Kennedy valued individuality and skill, and he charged poets with a great responsibility. This book, then, in its way, aspires to bear witness to his faith in "a world which will be safe not only for democracy and diversity but also for personal distinction."

With the exception of Abraham Lincoln, no president has inspired so much good poetry. Whether any of the poems in this book will endure is for others to determine. We hope that this book will be a beginning, that more fine Kennedy poems will be forthcoming, and that they will be widely read. For, as John F. Kennedy said of Robert Frost: "A nation reveals itself not only by the men it produces but also by the men it honors, the men it remembers."

ERWIN A. GLIKES
PAUL SCHWABER

August 1964

FOR JOHN F. KENNEDY HIS INAUGURATION

Gift Outright of "The Gift Outright"

With Some Preliminary History in Rhyme

Summoning artists to participate
In the august occasions of the state
Seems something artists ought to celebrate.
Today is for my cause a day of days.
And his be poetry's old-fashioned praise
Who was the first to think of such a thing.
This verse that in acknowledgment I bring
Goes back to the beginning of the end
Of what had been for centuries the trend;
A turning point in modern history.
Colonial had been the thing to be
As long as the great issue was to see
What country'd be the one to dominate
By character, by tongue, by native trait,
The new world Christopher Columbus found.
The French, the Spanish, and the Dutch were downed
And counted out. Heroic deeds were done.
Elizabeth the First and England won.
Now came on a new order of the ages
That in the Latin of our founding sages
(Is it not written on the dollar bill
We carry in our purse and pocket still?)
God nodded his approval of as good.
So much those heroes knew and understood,
I mean the great four, Washington,
John Adams, Jefferson, and Madison,—
So much they knew as consecrated seers
They must have seen ahead what now appears,

They would bring empires down about our ears
And by the example of our Declaration
Make everybody want to be a nation.
And this is no aristocratic joke
At the expense of negligible folk.
We see how seriously the races swarm
In their attempts at sovereignty and form.
They are our wards we think to some extent
For the time being and with their consent,
To teach them how Democracy is meant.
"New order of the ages" did we say?
If it looks none too orderly today,
'Tis a confusion it was ours to start
So in it have to take courageous part.
No one of honest feeling would approve
A ruler who pretended not to love
A turbulence he had the better of.
Everyone knows the glory of the twain
Who gave America the aeroplane
To ride the whirlwind and the hurricane.
Some poor fool has been saying in his heart
Glory is out of date in life and art.
Our venture in revolution and outlawry
Has justified itself in freedom's story
Right down to now in glory upon glory.
Come fresh from an election like the last,
The greatest vote a people ever cast,
So close yet sure to be abided by,
It is no miracle our mood is high.
Courage is in the air in bracing whiffs
Better than all the stalemate an's and ifs.
There was the book of profile tales declaring
For the emboldened politicians daring
To break with followers when in the wrong,
A healthy independence of the throng,
A democratic form of right divine
To rule first answerable to high design.

There is a call to life a little sterner,
And braver for the earner, learner, yearner.
Less criticism of the field and court
And more preoccupation with the sport.
It makes the prophet in us all presage
The glory of a next Augustan age
Of a power leading from its strength and pride,
Of young ambition eager to be tried,
Firm in our free beliefs without dismay,
In any game the nations want to play.
A golden age of poetry and power
Of which this noonday's the beginning hour.

"THE GIFT OUTRIGHT"

The land was ours before we were the land's.
She was our land more than a hundred years
Before we were her people. She was ours
In Massachusetts, in Virginia,
But we were England's, still colonials,
Possessing what we still were unpossessed by,
Possessed by what we now no more possessed.
Something we were withholding made us weak
Until we found out that it was ourselves
We were withholding from our land of living,
And forthwith found salvation in surrender.
Such as we were we gave ourselves outright
(The deed of gift was many deeds of war)
To the land vaguely realizing westward,
But still unstoried, artless, unenhanced,
Such as she was, such as she would become.

FOOTNOTE TO LORD ACTON

While in the Convention they were nominating the Next
    President of the United States,
I thought of death:
Not merely that ambition is a skull
And all microphones handles of a coffin;
Not merely that those former public speakers Socrates and
    Caesar
Are less than the moth's foot,
That grass is all power,
And only the absolute worm corrupts absolutely—

    Since on the rostrum they know this,
    In the galleries where they clutch staffs and banners
      they know this,
    The Next President of the United States knows this,
    Having for an example
    If not Koheleth
    Then the Past Presidents of the United States.

The forgotten speaker,
The alternate delegate,
The trampled demonstrator,
The shunned and shunted eldest statesman with his honed wail
    unheard,
How irrelevant is death to the pieties of men!

Death the dark, dark horse.

July 1960

FLORENCE VICTOR

BERLIN CRISIS

The dentist drilled for two-and-one-half hours.
When I left, the President was telling us
About Berlin. The doctor said: "At least
We'll have our teeth filled."
                                    Outside, in the heat,
I slung myself along the main street of our town.
"I'm missing the speech! I'm missing the speech!"
And then, from all the cars and store-fronts,
Jack's odd twang harangued the night. "America,"
I thought, and felt so safe I was ashamed.

July 25, 1961

12

NO RETREAT

I am in earnest. I will not equivocate. I will not excuse. I will not retreat a single inch. I will be heard. —PRESIDENT KENNEDY, QUOTING WILLIAM LLOYD GARRISON

We who must write GM a stinging letter
About the defective fuel tank on our Buick,
Who must purchase for baby a lightweight, foldable, washable,
Nylon-mesh-with-aluminum-buttons playpen,
And spread on our lawn a non-toxic lawn-food miracle;

Who've just been considering renting a Tuckaway cottage
Complete with a fibre-glass cruiser sleeping four
For July, and possibly August, on the North Shore,
Where the nights are cool and the Club has a weekly
        smorgasbord;

Who plan to subscribe next fall to the *Kiplinger Newsletter*
And to take a week off for a cultural fling at Christmas
At the theaters (off-Broadway) and the U.N. (maybe)—

In earnest are we
In Geneva, Seoul, Jakarta, Karachi, Macao and (of course)
        West Germany;

Nor equivocate nor excuse will
In Amoy, Saigon, Llasa, Lambeth, Laos and Leopoldville:

Nor retreat
(If a case should arise) from Lemnos, Naxos, Chios, Sicily,
        Pantellaria, Malta or Crete;

But will heard be
From London, Paris, Rome, Athens, Vienna, Warsaw,
        Budapest, Prague, Moscow, Omsk and New Delhi
To ultima Thule.

September 1961

13

GEORGE HITCHCOCK

MR. KENNEDY PROPOSES TO PACIFY THE CARIBBEANS

Recalling the manicured nails on the mandolin
the subtle vials of *eau de cologne*
mignonette rouge the chaste scarves
and the varieties of predictable haemophilia
    we await the angels.

Foreseeing the doves with turrets and *démarches*
the bonewhite beach and the flight of watches
the palmettoes suddenly ambulant
and the strange petals with their odoriferous cries
    we await the angels.

Anticipating iron colloquies in the cloudless sky
the exchange of roses in the vestibule
the fury the glass the splintered tongue
the brick the ash the dispersal of seed
    we await the angels.

November 1962

14

JONATHAN WILLIAMS

DAVENPORT GAP

the tulip poplar is not a
poplar it is a magnolia:
liriodendron tulipifera.

the young grove on the eastern slopes of
Mt Cammerer reminds me
of the two huge trees
at Monticello, favorites
of Mr Jefferson;

and of the Virginia lady
quoting Mr Kennedy:
the recent gathering of
Nobel Prize Winners at the
White House—the most
brilliant assemblage
in that dining room
since Mr Jefferson
dined there
alone . . .

a liriodendron
wind, a liriodendron
mind

May 1962

15

LONG LINES

At twenty thousand feet—the earth below was overcast—
the top of the cloud was like a desert flat lightly dusted with snow
and I at the sunny porthole agreed to be resigned
as in a bright hospital where they would feed me well,
but like one peacefully dying rather than convalescent.
The blue sky was immense to its skim-milky horizon
and the sun glorious as if awash and wet
with its light I stared at hungrily with my own streaming eyes.
Then were my cares for my sick country quieted
though not forgotten, and the unhappy loneliness
in which I ever live was quieted.
Dimly I briefly saw below the wide meandering
among the Blue Ridge Mountains Shenandoah River
and again! one friendly sparkle from a wave
like a signal to me leaped across four miles of space
saying "God! God!" or "Man! Man!" or "Death!"
or whatever it was, very pleasantly.

November 21, 1963

16

NOVEMBER 22, 1963

Morning; the slow rising of a cold sun.
Outside of town the suburbs, crosshatched and wan,
Lie like the fingers of some hand. In one
Of these, new, nondescript, an engine starts,
A car door slams, a man drives off. Its gates
Bannered, streets flagged and swept, the city waits.

Dallas

RICHARD O'CONNELL

NEKROS

It slouched at the window changing
Changing its shape and its skin
It clung at the window changing

It seemed like a centipede
It seemed like a huge centipede
Or serpent or strange dragon

How many incarnations?

Forty times it changed
Forty times until this . . .
Still it kept changing
And still it stayed there changing
Convulsing inside of itself
In hideous suffering
This selv-slaughtering thing

Forty incarnations.
And what did it become next?

I saw it shedding its clothes . . .
I saw it dropping its flesh
In a small green public place . . .
Sunlight . . . by a fountain
Its unintelligible body
Gleaming dark and wet

Then this shape was a man's?

Maybe a man's, I don't know

And what worse thing to tell?

18

A head dropped back and dying
Pouring blood from its skull . . .
All history stark in that flow

BULLETIN

Is dead. Is dead. How all
The radios sound the same.
That static is our seed.
Is dead. We heard. Again.

We peck at the words like bran
Strung on a string of air.
Is dead. Again. Is dead.
Too rhythmic for despair.

Our faces are all the same,
Learning to taste the word.
Lockjawed with awkwardness.
Is dead. We know. We heard.

LEWIS TURCO

NOVEMBER 22, 1963

Weeping, I write this. You are dead. The dark
animal of the heart, the beast that bides
stilly in its web of flesh, has stolen
flight again out of the air. What is there
to say? That I wish we were gods? That the
mind of man were equal to his lusts? It
is not—not yet. You were a man, but more:
you were an idea dreamt in a sweet
hour while the spider slept. We make our
web: its habitant makes greatness of its
prey. We are ourselves victim and victor.
You were and are ourselves. In killing you
we murder an emblem of what we strive
to be: not men, but Man. In mourning you,
good Man, we grieve for what we are, not what
we may become.
               Sleep, my heart. We will try
Once more. Sleep, sleep, John. We will try again.

GWENDOLYN BROOKS

THE ASSASSINATION OF JOHN F. KENNEDY

. . . this Good, this Decent, this Kindly man. . . .
—SENATOR MANSFIELD

I hear things crying in the world.
A nightmare congress of obscure
Delirium uttering overbreath
The tilt and jangle of this death.

Who had a sense of world and man,
Who had an apt and antic grace
Lies lenient, lapsed and large beneath
The tilt and jangle of this death.

The world goes on with what it has.
Its reasoned, right and only code.
Coaxing, with military faith,
The tilt and jangle of this death.

BEFORE THE SABBATH

The man is gone on a Friday.
Good father of silence,
give us peace of the Sabbath
with promises you grow in our blood.
Gone on a Friday before the Sabbath
of rest, his blood on stretchers
and on surgical instruments,
nowhere growing a promise,
the instruments cold, the forehead mute.
Good father of emptiness,
you keep saying over and over
in the birth of children
that we are not born to die,
but the mind is dulled,
for the man is gone on a Friday
before the Sabbath of the world remade.
Smiling, he is dead,
too quickly to explain.

By a hand in defiance
the fine, warm sun has been extinguished,
by one of us, talking of anger
and frustration. In the sudden darkness
the structures going up stand agape.
In unfinished corners we huddle,
growing cold.

FRONTIER

Daniel Boone stepped up to a window
(What! a window?) with his trusty rifle,
And he shot his bear.
This was some bear.
It was a millionaire,
A Harvard, London, and a South Sea bear
A French, a football bear.

A corporate family
And incorporate party
Thoroughly transistized
Into his rocking chair
Built and bureaucratized,
Daddied and deared and dared,
Indomitable bear.

What an investment
Of time, of love too,
All in one body,
A computation
Of maximal purpose,
A one man world.

Daniel is angry
That after the eighth grade
This bear should travel
So far ahead.
Unfair
That a bear
Should rock so big a chair.

So gets him, and as he is got
Shows him

24

Shows us
It takes no complicated bomb or plot
To win again us back to wilderness,
But just one pot- pure, individual -shot.

IN IDENTITY

As difference blends into identity
Or blurs into obliteration, we give
To zero our position at the center,
Withdraw our belief and baggage.

As rhyme at the walls lapses, at frontiers
Customs scatter like a flight of snow,
And boundaries moonlike draw us out, our opponents
Join us, we are their refuge.

As barriers between us melt, I may treat you
Unkindly as myself, I may forget
Your name as my own. Then enters
Our anonymous assailant.

As assonance by impulse burgeons
And that quaver shakes us by which we are spent,
We may move to consume another with us,
Stir into parity another's cyphers.

Then when our sniper steps to a window
In the brain, starts shooting, and we fall surprised,
Of what we know not do we ask forgiveness
From ourselves, for ourselves?

JOURNALS NOV. 22, '63

The black & white glare blink in the inky Air Force night
as the Helikopter rose straight up in the television frame
carrying President Johnson toward the newsphoto White House
past the tail flag of the giant United States of America super-jet
settled at rest and lonesome under the klieg light field
swarmed with cops brass photographers mikrophones blip
                                                Macnamara chill
Long nosed Oswald suspect in Dallas of half mast pro Castro
                                                assassination.

DOROTHY GILBERT

AT THE BROOKLYN DOCKS

November 23, 1963

In the morning air, the freighter *Havskar*,
From Oslo, lies drawn up at her Brooklyn pier.
The light breaks on her masts and ropes, and shows
Their endless tents and triangles that crowd
In the white air, and rise and ride each other.
A man waves, and a boom descends; a shout,
And a crate is hoisted up from dock to decks.
It swings and lands, and the men on board take it away.
Near me, above the ships, the workmen spread
Tar on the roofs, black in the early sun.
The smell of sea water and tar is thick;
It stings in the nostrils, and, like coffee, wakes me.

Wakes me to what I see and what I know.
Where the light strikes, there is the thrust of sadness,
Up the white spars and ropes, the shapes of day,
Along the decks, and on the *Havskar's* flag,
At half-mast, like her neighbors' and my own.
Is work as old as grief? Watching, I feel
The slow and wounded groping of my senses
Toward my old life. Here, in my neighborhood,
Under the flags lost among ropes, the men
Cry out, crates swing in the silence after,
Under the watchful eyes the burden lands.
All down the shore, the day changes and moves.

DONALD HALL

SPIDER HEAD

the spider glints
he is huge he is made of aluminium
slowly the crane lowers him
outside a glass building
his legs crawl in the air
he dangles turning
by a steel thread
the sun splits on his metal skin
no one sees him

I kneel at a wooden box
in shade in silence
eye-socket touches felt eyepiece
a car rolls slowly
into the crossed hairs
a head
enters the segments of a circle
hairs cross on a head
I squeeze slowly

the crane lifts the spider slowly
his legs retracting
he becomes a sphere a point
glinting aluminium
no one sees him
the crane swerves him over a ledge
his nest on a high building
humming in a cement hole
electric glass

KENNEDY UCCISO

Don't scream at me you God damn' wops,
nine at night. I know what the headline says.
Blasted by some creep in Dallas.
Don't ask me who Johnson is.
Don't ask *racismo, comunismo?*
I don't know. That fountain lit
and flowing over naked ladies, fish,
animals and birds, is blurred. You and words
in giant print keep banging at my head.

I voted for him, not my kind of man.
My kind could not be president,
just a target for the cold. You slip in
noisy knives of why. *Un gran uomo?*
Certamente. I know, here this very year.
Yes, a Catholic. Yes. Yes. Very rich.
A man who put some sixty million lives
on some vague line and won.
I'd vote for him again. But here
in the *piazza* where the fountain
makes wet love to ladies and stone swans
I want your questions and my hate to end.

The fountain runs in thighs of lovely stone.
Ladies do quite well, subduing swans
and lizards, giving in to fish. You Romans,
quite *simpatici.* Someday we'll be you.
I weep in the *piazza*, perfect wop.
Take your questions to a sainted star.
My Italian fails. *Come si dice:*
He was not afraid of what we are.

29

WILLIAM BUTLER

NOVEMBER 25, 1963

Drums, drums, I too am dead.
I breathe no breath, but only dread.
I have no soul, but lay my head
Upon his soul, and on that bed
I stop.

Drums in heartbeat cadence drill
His life away. My life is still.
My heart drums down my wit, my will,
And with his cadence, mounts the hill
And stops.

He stops. I stop. He ends. I end.
He will not heal. I will not mend.
He goes alone. I take no friend.
His God is mine. He kneels. I bend.
All stops.

And that is all of me tonight.
I do not want tomorrow's light.
I do not want the sound or sight
Of time. No more. These words I write,
And stop.

INSTEAD OF AN ELEGY

Bullets blot out the Life-Time smile,
Apollo of the picture-page,
Blunt-faced young lion
    Caught by vile
Death in an everlasting cage:

And, no more young men in the world,
The old men troop to honour him.
The drums beat glum,
    Slight snow is swirled
In dazzling sun, pale requiem.

And pale dark-veiled Persephone,
A golden child in either hand,
Stands by white pillars;
    Silently,
It seems she might for ever stand.

In bright grey sun, processionals
Of pomp and honour, and of grief,
Crown that dead head
    With coronals.
Some stony hearts feel some relief:

But not your heart, America,
Beating so slow and sure and strong,
Stricken in his
    Triumphal car,
Guard Caesar's bitter laurels long

With soldiers' music, rites of war:
He had proved bravely when put on!
The soldiers shoot.
    Rage echoes far
Above the grave at Arlington.

HISTORY

(i. m. J. F. K.)

I am a monster.
Among small
crouching years,
I take up

Death in my hand
and Death shakes
wild as a shrew.
I pile bones

high by the wall.
I eat graves.
Chanting,
they bring me
graves to eat.

ELEGY FOR THE NEW YEAR

1

Dulled by the news, all day I keep behind
The curtains of my room. They will have to do
In keeping my dried-out self
From falling through the air like a leaf
As the year tapers to a close.
This is the legendary season
When the young die sooner than the old.

2

Calm as a hurricane's eye,
My T.V. set in black and white
Stares unblinking at Washington—
Pearly, spacious, dazzled with shock—
Where under a sky of cold
Lingering Confederate grey,
A stallion, Black Jack, tosses
And snorts, spirited as your soul
Gone from this world, ours by default.

3

America stops turning over her conscience,
Halved these hundred years like Hamlet's,
And clutches her flag's reopened wound
Running red through the bandages.
In a sky swept clean of cherry blossoms,
She seems to see a future drained
Of all color but black and white, alternatives.
White Christmas come,
The Union will twinkle

Like a child, her arms full of gifts,
Pretending all is well.

4

Someone who has dreamed his father dead,
And stepped away from the dream, holding
His breath like a shoe in each hand,
Comes to himself, a honeycomb of fear,
Each cell a nursery weeping for home;
Hears the wind tiptoe from door to door and whisper,
"There is no place to be homesick for. You're free."
A soul winging like a gunshot
Through the ether's paper bag,
Beyond sight, beyond recognition . . . breaking apart,
Wrings an old restlessness from me,
Heart all aflutter for the take-off.

MICHAEL GOLDMAN

THE PROBES

Let us section his nude body
into five stages,
each by a cut through the groin.

The eye that seems to stare at you
from the open hip is
illusion; it is a slice of your eye.

The choric knotting of the dark ropes
is like slow thinking;
we reach the chipped bulges of the joints.

The massive thigh-bone now, the temple, the great
hangar of the chest, the
facial plane stripped clean by a rotary saw.

Here the examining knife
comes on softness, on
pockets of fluid that explode.

An arm borne by the sewage!
Heart's splendor;
a king's mouth smashed to grinning rocks.

Quickly we return to the scrape of metal
over bone. The wiping-up
continues. I feel the

cool touch of a sponge on the back of my neck.
What do you feel?
Do you feel we have just about covered the subject?

35

Then let us finish off our operations
neatly by felicitating
Language—who has survived so many changes

of state, of policy, of conversation,
with no loss to herself. It's so
swell to feel superior, even to a nation.

THE SPONTANEOUS MAN,
THE GIFTED ASSASSIN

The spontaneous man, the gifted assassin
lies down in our sleep tonight.
In nervous weather, a cold nation
settling inward, meets hate

rising like an athlete from his pool,
smiling, flicking the water from his chest.
On the stone steps the water smears like oil.
He is naked; we are impressed.

36

BELIEF

1

drums gather and humble us beyond escape,
propound the single, falling fact:
time, suspended between memory and present,
hangs unmeasured, empty

2

erect,
disciplined by cadence into direction, the soldier
obeys the forms of rumor:
the riderless horse,
restive with the pressure of held flight,
tosses the hung bit,
worries the soldier's tameless arm—
sidling, prances the energy out

3

ahead, unalterable, the fact proceeds,
and the bit holds:
the fire-needle bites,
training the head on course

4

the light, determined rattle
of the caisson
breaking into sunlight
through the crystal black ribbons of trees!
the slack traces,
weightlessness at the shoulders of horses!

5

if we could break free
and run this knowledge out,
burst this energy of grief
through a hundred countrysides!
if black through the black night
we could outrun
this knowledge into a different morning!

6

belief, light as a drumrattle,
touches us and lifts us into tears.

JACQUELINE

And when she strides
soul uplifted
with unbrazen eyes,
his coffin cannot contain him,
her footsteps deliver him
in rhythms of dignity
down the avenues of our pulsedrums
that, mourning, we receive,
and, accepting his death, we
take unto us the living
flesh of his meanings.

NATIONAL COLD STORAGE COMPANY

The National Cold Storage Company contains
More things than you can dream of.
Hard by the Brooklyn Bridge it stands
In a litter of freight cars,
Tugs to one side; the other, the traffic
Of the Long Island Expressway.
I myself have dropped into it in seven years
Midnight tossings, plans for escape, the shakes.
Add this to the national total—
Grant's Tomb, the Civil War, Arlington,
The young President dead.
Above the warehouse and beneath the stars
The poets creep on the harp of the Bridge.
But see,
They fall into the National Cold Storage Company
One by one. The wind off the river is too cold,
Or the times too rough, or the Bridge
Is not a harp at all. Or maybe
A monstrous birth inside the warehouse
Must be fed by everything—ships, poems,
Stars, all the years of our lives.

UNTIL DEATH
DO US PART

To think of them
from afar
to think of the distance, that air
its broken voices

> thousands of miles, the sea
> and the rivers, returning
> the sun also rising
>> but then

it was less: the distance
two hundred yards! They are moving
into the sights, they are moving

> into the eye, wide open,
> opened in the earth
> his earth, to let him in

the suddenly opened eye
the windscreen meshed
into a honeycomb of light—

To think of them
as close: as he was

his head in her lap, her arm
across his chest
as they were floating, floating

> wherever it was
> we were going, we canot stay
> on the road

41

yet must drive on
and out of their sight who try
who tried to think of us, as we entered
the dark city

> to be encased in a light
> of diamonds and death,
> dead center of stillness

where there is
no fear
> out of their sights
each into his
her night, now shared
> forever.

D A B N E Y   S T U A R T

TOWARD COLONOS

for the death of John F. Kennedy

Think of this loss
As a trick of light

    The brute in us
    All taking abrupt shape
    In the quick darkness,
    For once the haphazard
    Labyrinth of our veins
    Stunned at its center
    By the still Minotaur,

    Or the terrific clarity
    When the bullets struck our eyes
    Like Jocaste's pins

A brilliant fleshing out
No word
Can hold a candle to.

FORMAL ELEGY

I

A hurdle of water, and O these waters are cold
(warm at outset) in the dirty end.
Murder on murder on murder, where I stagger,
whiten the good land where we have held out.
These kills were not for loot,
however Byzantium hovers in the mind:
were matters of principle—that's worst of all—
& fear & crazed mercy.
Ruby, with his mad claim
he shot to spare the Lady's testifying,
probably is sincere.
No doubt, in his still cell, his mind sits pure.

II

Yes. it looks like a wilderness—pacem appellant.
Honour to Patrolman Tippit. Peace to the rifler's widow.
Seven, I believe, play fatherless.

III

Scuppered the yachts, the choppers, big cars, jets.
Nobody goes anywhere,
lengthened (days) into TV.
I am four feet long, invisibly.
What in the end will be left of us is a stare,
underwater.
If you want me to join you in confident prayer, let's
not.
I sidled in & past, gazing upon it,
the bier.

44

IV

Too Andean hopes, now angry shade.—
I am an automobile. Into me climb
many, and go their ways. Onto him climbed
a-many and went his way.
For a while we seemed to be having a holiday
off from ourselves—ah, but the world is wigs,
as sudden we came to feel
and even his splendid hair kept not wholly real
fumbling & falsing in & out of the Bay of Pigs,
the bad moment of this excellent man,
suffered by me as a small car can.
Faithful to course we stayed.

V

Some in their places are constrained to weep.
Stunned, more, though.
Black foam. A weaving snake. An invulnerable sleep.
It doing have to come so.
All at once, hurtless, in the tide of applause
& expectation. I write from New York
where except for a paraplegic exterminator—
a gracious & sweet guy—
nobody has done no work
lately

VI

It's odd perhaps that Dallas   cannot after their crimes
criminals protect or Presidents.
Fat Dallas, a fit set.
I would not perhaps have voted for him next time.
Images of Mr Kennedy blue the air,
who is little now, with no chance to grow great,
but who have set his touch across the State,
true-intended, strong

VII

My breath comes heavy, does my breath.
I feel heavy about the President's death.

VIII

I understand I hear I see I read
schoolgirls in Dallas when the white word came
or slammed, cheered in their thoughtful grades,
brought-up to a loving tone.
I do not sicken but somewhat with shame
I shift my head an inch; who are my own.
I have known a loving Texas   woman in parades
and she was boastful & treacherous.
That boringest of words, whereas here I blush,
"education," peters to a nailing of us.

IX

An editor has asked me in my name
what wish or prophecy I'd like to state
for the new year. I am silent on these occasions
steadily, having no love for a fool
(which I keep being) but I break my rule:
I do all-wish the bullets swim astray
sent to the President, and that all around
help, and his heart keep sound.
I have a strange sense

                he's about to be the best of men.
Amen.

X

It's quiet at Arlington. Rock Creek is quiet.
My primers, with Mount Auburn. Everybody should
have his sweet boneyards. Yet let the young not go,

46

our apprentice King! Alas,
muffled, he must. He seemed good:
brainy in riot, daring, cool.
                              So
let us abandon the scene of disorder. Drop
them shattered bodies into tranquil places,
where moulder as you will. We compose our faces
cold as the cresting waters; ready again.
The waters break.
All black & white together, stunned, survive
the final insolence to the head of you;
bow.
Overwhelmed-un, live.
A rifle fact is over, pistol facts
almost entirely are too.
The man of a wise face opened it to speak:
Let us continue.

CAUSE & EFFECT

Am *I* the bullet,
or the target,
or the hand
that holds the gun?
Or the whisper
in the brain saying *Aim, Fire?*
Is the bullet innocent though it kill?
Must the target stand unblinking and still?
Can one escape, the other stop, if it will?
Will the trigger-finger obey through force?
If the hand reverse command,
will the pregnant gun abort its curse?
The brain, surely *it* can refrain—
unclench the gun, break open
the pod of murder,
let the target rise and run.
But first the whisper must be caught,
before the shot—
the single wasp be burnt out,
before the nest, infested, swarms with
the multiple thought—
each sting the trigger pressed!

GEORGE DEKKER

22nd NOVEMBER, 1963

Had not each distant good
Much nearer evil stirred,
Had those who should have, stood,
Might you have kept your word?

For the best, you thought, delay:
Be politic, though just;
Keep violence at bay;
Act firmly, when you must.

Now violence behind
A telescopic sight
Shapes the future to its mind.
Kennedy, you were right.

And you were much maligned.

STANLEY KOEHLER

IN ARLINGTON CEMETERY

In the city of memorials,
among tombstones and small
headstones, I look through the cold
not for a monument
but for a grave with ferns
and evergreens lent
from the season past. A flame burns
in the air, not a leaf
to shelter it, blown like our grief,
variable and new, endless and old.

Uphill, over open ground,
on the wind's edge are coming
echoes of drummers drumming
on tight-stretched skin,
tattooing the stillness
to the funeral sound
of hoofs at the hobble,
unharnessed, held in
to the ritual pace;
and of wheels on the cobble.

The carriage circles a green park
with its temple, the dark
porch where the Form in his chair
sheds a marble tear
for what is fated like him:
statues for whom
there are robes of stone.
Love waves in her car
while Hate takes aim
through a lens from far-

off, and History bleeds, an old charade,
and Madmen fly
the line of parade
down empty walks, and from the shocked
stage the Actor's shout
is driven out.
Still, in those marble eyes
deepgrained as memory,
the barns are burning, the streets are blocked,
while motorcade and obsequies

through iron gates
to somber guns and the horn's last notes
continually come.
For this to end, for the drum
to be stilled at last,
more than this green bough
will be cut and cast.

The flame leaps up. Fresh as our vow,
it makes a gentle monument at night
with the simplicity of light.

RICHARD BARKER

NIGHT OF THE PRESIDENT'S FUNERAL

Sixty thousand faces go dark on the Strip
I come home 3 strangers in whiteface
are smashing my walls &
there's blood on my pillow
splinters of glass!
splinters of glass!

Dead Verlaine
hangs in the closet, fingers
trail from his wings. His
unlovely bald head
is a dirty vermilion
& he eats the hawk's ripe leavings.

A rain of crutches outside the window
Janet throws knives at her husbands.
These are the others
they are your brothers
of course he was killed.

PHILIP BOOTH

THANKSGIVING 1963

She walks a beach assaulted by the sea.
Gray waves horse the tide ashore. He

sails far out, alone, beyond retreat.
The muffled sea drums slowly on her heart.

She walks against a wind that never sleeps.
The sea originates and ends. She keeps

the beachhead, reining in an empty horse.
Her beachfire keeps long ships on their long course.

Now may she sleep by how the slow sea breaks.
And finally weep, this night of our dark thanks.

OUT OF THE WEST
OF LUCKY RIDERS

Out of the West of lucky riders
On breakneck horses
Who land upright, who plunge
Into safe rivers,
Get winged once in the arm
Then flicker into sunset,
Out of the West came death.
>   *Dark mother always gliding near*
>   *With soft feet.*
A wild West death,
A shot and a slumping down
And the horse crazed with fear
Charging over the cliff,
Stallion hooves still beating,
But on air now, floating;
Pegasus suspended, falling . . .
Then the hollow sound.
>   *O death, I cover you over*
>   *With roses and early lilies.*
Word spreading through town,
Men and women calling,
Children running to hear.
Then the silent knots of people,
And one bell tolling:
Autumn's flags slowly dropping
Toward the luckless winter ahead
With no surprise of hooves.
>   *O sane and sacred death,*
>   *Over the treetops I float thee a song.*
Townsman and stranger, come
Take this death in your arms,
Lift it to your shoulders, easy now.

54

Carry it past the town,
Carry it past the ravine,
Raise it to the mesa, easy now.
Easy now.
Make a mound of stones.
Leave it to the sun.
A death came out of the West.

Let the legend begin.

J.F.K.

To pierce through power
To the living things that make it, to youth
In the old poet, to anger

Cold as death's eyes upon it,
To science patient amid armed lies,
To truth that needs

A second voice—
This was your mind's strength, torn from us,
Spilled by the blind bullet.

Can the world die as a man dies,
And mankind stumble to death?
Can the star-years spun into mind,
Mind spun into freedom, be lost,
And time inhuman, and space
Manless, wink to the dark?

Death draws from a man
All but the light he has won; there he stands
Unshadowed, the brave stance, smiling,
The bitter joy of days fought,
And the love of the new day upon him; there
Visited well
By all faithful hopes,
Let him stand, his country-to-be alive in his eyes.

AUDREY MC GAFFIN

FINAL PROCESSION
for John Fitzgerald Kennedy

Suddenly in sunlight
A shadow. Slack folds
Of the banner of state
Formed on that moving coffin
A black arrow.

As suddenly wind
Came. The arrow broken
Flag snapping
Passed. O impermanent state
Not perilous now . . .

LORENZO THOMAS

NOT THAT HURRIED GRIEF
for John F. Kennedy (d. 1963)

1

You were only a grainy face in the newspapers
A briefly passionate figure of speech
During breakfast   The voice of the radio at the end
Of my hand, your reputation

Didn't gleam as much as the fork in my hand
Such memorial! Your life was nothing
To me your death though an inscrutable mark on the lintel,
The same world I live in

I think of the popular word "transitory"
Oh! At least it should bend
My heart   but I am only distressed and mistrustful
On the bus everybody weeping around me

I think of the popular word "transitory"
Your funeral, watching it on tv
I think the cathode overburdened, the gray lines strained
Your funeral lost in air

Our world so badly fitted for permanence
Or sorrow, your widow lost in air
Your name lonely on highways and airports   At least
You did not die to be a battleship

2

What kind of poverty becomes me, a callous wretch
I think of the popular word "transitory"
And I am saddened for you   Oh, we stinge on ourselves!

I think of the word "callous"
And I know it's antique   I watched your funeral, your
          widow moving
Like a Gloucester woman across the small screen
The jet planes our gesture of reverence,
And I was strangely moved, a genuinely new emotion, not
That hurried grief
                    flags drooping in the dark
As I walked along East 70th street
The night you died prim doormen bland and perfectly usual
Such memorial! Your death an oblique fact
You do not come to mind on the street
The airport has only a dim recollection, the times you
          landed there
And we are not ashamed
The airport your memorial has no eyes, no mouth
My mouth fallow of grief is plains in the western movie
          the night you died
What is this "I am going to the movies"
Barbara crying that afternoon and you flying back to Washington
Now we are sitting alone in our strange world, our
          curiosities assuaged
By scientific films of growing flowers in the southwest
Forgive the distance that couldn't fit me to appropriate weeds
The weeds on your grave, my replacement

BARBARA HOWES

A NIGHT PICTURE
OF POWNAL

for J. F. K.

Thanks to the moon,
Branches of our trees are coral
Fans, cast on the lanky snow
Which, crusted though,

Takes impressions
As Matthew Brady's eye received
The desperation of Civil War;
He was its retina

And watched history
Rise and set. Above its kilt
Of steel-blue air the moon turns,
A circle leans

To stare down fissures
Of space to that black forest set
Like matchsticks on the white hillside;
All sound has died.

Our apple tree
Prints its own photograph, its strong
Branches espaliered on the snow
Fading, will not go

From our minds, the clean
Etching of dark on white, each detail
Tuned to the whole; in its precision
Enduring as bone.

What we have seen
Has become history; tragedy
Marks its design upon the brain—
We are stained by its stain.

ROBERT HOLLANDER

NOVEMBER 22, 1963

You and the hoary poet
In the wind in Washington
Talking of power and poetry
Didn't know a fool had been taught
That he could shoot and read,
Send fathers falling on top of their sons
Seeing your ruined familiar head.

The tragic lesson of tragedies
That good men are schooled to go wronged
Is not the mere game of tragedians
But of the ever Iago
And of his ever fellow,
The good-hearted and headstrong
And always tendered Othello.

THOMAS WHITBREAD

NOVEMBER 25, 1963

The assassination of the President,
Among its many effects, confers upon
The slightest act a clarity of precision.
The sharpening of a pencil with a knife,
My old Scout knife, twenty years old, today
Sharply reseen as its invented self.
The cutting of my nails with old small scissors,
Trying, as always, not to hurt the quick.
Then encountering, taking up the pencil,
Tooth marks, not mine, and breaking it in half
In the frustration of rage, despair, and grief
At life not being as it ought to be.
She bit it. Our love should be alive, as he
Much more should be, and stupidly is not.

ROBERT HAZEL

GUARD OF HONOR

West to Dallas

Leave the flattering libraries, the graceful Eastern towns.
Leave the untold beads and the uncounted leaves of grass.
Leave the blue panes of cathedrals, the red leather of law,
     the white silence of poetry.
Take yourself to Texas in an open car.
Be for one moment the advertised Zero of infantile people:
     rich boy in a big car, hair wild, teeth clean:
     young god without wound.

West is the place to die; it stands for death.
No law except chance and impulse in that country:
          land blazing and sterile, cold with the howls
          of sun-crazed and moon-frozen animals
          with torn fur, then sun on the carcasses.
West is the place to die, my President.

By day in a freeway
cavalcade of sunburnt limousines,
you ran the gauntlet of leather and lead.
On the thin fabric of law between reason and chaos
you laid your head,
blood on the temple, then sound of a rifle
          swaddled in oil.
Hungry hands were waving.
A Negro woman wept into her purse.

Riderless Horse

From Andrews Field you ride into the Capital.
A guard of honor escorts your sudden corpse
        down an aluminum ladder.
Your widow stalks your body through an avenue
of bare sycamores, and one answering bell,
leading heads of state to altar and precipice.
On the birthday of your son, your widow
walks bars of a dirge on the pavement
        towards fountain and abyss.
Among swords of sunlight drawn by the spokes
        of the caisson
and the white manes of horses, she walks
        into noon and midnight.
Above the muffled drums,
the high voice of a young soldier
tells the white horses how slow to go
before your widow and children, walking
behind the flag-anchored coffin—
and one riderless black horse dancing!

Widow

And so she took a ring from her finger and placed it in his hands.
        —SENATOR MANSFIELD

Let her take his blood
        on her tongue,
his being wine
        at her green altar,
the sacrament of summer
        in her veins.
Heal her, her children
        with books and duties,

65

with winter land for walking,
        a child in her arms,
and no office
        except the natural care
of fall weeds bending,
        left, driven.
And may she be
        fall, weeds, all
beauty's luck and fullness.
        Heal, make her well
with my country's bloom.
        Let her have to know
and not learn again.

Supplication of the Poor

Bipartisan committees of the Congress hail
        the hearse into Pennsylvania Avenue
Men in the Congress who were blinded by your vision
        and refused your living acts
pave the long route of your cortege
        with sanctimonious lies—
always the machinery for plunder and blood,
        not yours then or now.

The market rises and falls.
Rich men pay little taxes.
Lack-law rules.
The substance is eaten.
The husks drift in the wind.
My President, where can we go?
Into what country
where the white-poor and the black-poor
do not have to barter dignity for bread?

66

The Post-Christian Era: an Oration

But the witless prayers of children in the dark
    must ebb into silence.
The eunuchs of Rome and New York must burn their robes.
The violent and guilty boyhood of nations
    carrying rifles and crosses
    must end and be forgotten.

All the sacred emblems
    of religious awe, of tribal arrogance
    that have killed you
    must be laid down:
    the plowshares that were beaten into swords,
    the sacred wine-drops molded into bullets,
    the blinding cores of atoms
    that have killed you—
    all must be buried.

The creation of gods to forgive
the evil in men,
the orgies of guilt and expiation,
must be left behind in the same way
men once shed the long hair from their bodies
and lost their fangs.

Let them lay all their rings and weapons,
with their archaic beauty and terror,
on your grave.

Light at Arlington

At Arlington the fall sunlight dies.
Across the dark Potomac, Lincoln sits, hands on stone knees.

At Arlington no steel or silver, no sword or chalice will remain
　　clear as your eyes.

President I love as my grandfather loved Lincoln,
in the silence after the bugle, lie down.
Lie in your forest of stone.
Lie close to Lincoln.

On the dark hill a flower of light is blooming
　　clear as your eyes were.

GEORGE CUOMO

THE MAN OF MY DREAMS

The wild man that last night I dreamed
Now sleeps to dream of me.
This morning in his fantasy
I do not bother him:
Nothing dismays this confessor.

And which is worse—to watch
His simpering acrobatics
Or prance for him the way
He dreams me to, balancing globes
On my nose and whipping
Flesh that perhaps awake I love?

Last night his shrieks were raw as glass;
Though he sweats and stinks, flares
Red with riot, I know
He is armed, and cool, and can aim.

I, assured by the morning news,
Scrape jars for daily fare,
While he, random as a lobster,
Writes our history.

FIVE POEMS FOR J.F.K.

Reading Buber

Words escape me, I face a loss
Feel absences, the moon's weight.
I am chalk, the skies behind me;
Growth of it, catastrophe, the world's fate.
I am silent, at ease. Trust only, I pause.
          "History," one says,
"Is an approach," the succession of sounds—
Myself at that point in it that I know,
Holding of the breath in the dark.

That It That Thing   Light

Night, light and the night, light
Sails that were not clouds/but sails—
The wind was who a thing I believed
Sails, that it that thing
Light, that wind, gave rise
Itself, to Night, light and the night, light,
I, O stone. The world is fact, light
Who ever more holy sails   I dream.

70

Celebration

Outside, the snow on a low
Black stock car. Its side collapsed,
There is the outline
Of a numeral, rusted 8 or 9.
Across from us an old man
            reads Gray's *Anatomy*.
Christmas bells on the P.A. system,
Cars gliding on packed ice,
Sounds of the Short Line buses.

Dec. '63

The talk is of Johnson and a Congress
Which has done nothing. The accents are
Of Virginia, Maryland, the whining
South. I sit in the back booth of a Chinese
            restaurant,
Washington, 1963. Before me lie
The New York Times, some old classwork
And a journal I carry everywhere.
I am bemused, distracted even.
All over things fly in and out of windows.
Roaches run up and back across the floor.
What is there to object to? I drink beer
And eat Chinese fortune cookies.
I am heartened. The revelation is at hand.
Old classwork, objects on a table;
All landscapes, the murals and tapestries—

It is time to go home now. The new snow,
Slush, the dark. Our seven children, my three wives

71

Wait for me. Already I am embracing them,
The snow upon me, pockets full of presents,
Certainty, groceries. I am, on the whole,
In step with the new Administration.

Poem

The rocks dark, green as leaves. Moss clings
To them, as if to a belief in them.
                              Breathes.

LINES FOR A PRESIDENT

I. The Inauguration and Shortly After

You could not stop the snow the sky dumped down,
The cold, the lectern smoking when the priest
Invoked the Lord. Did the Lord in answer jab
Your poet blind? Was that your high silk hat
They held against the sun for Robert Frost?
And still he could not see his words for you.
Coatless, then, as if winter were not here
You blow cold words, your hand chops air.

Your wife's French chef breaks skulls
Of eggs. Upstairs an attendant
Gardens in her hair.
A maid brings scented pearls,
The world of Louis and Molière,
Her conquest of Versailles
And Athens. Downstairs
You praise the Spartans.

II. At the Funeral

Let all those who would stop a war
Sit in a chair and rock,
And stare at a woman with flowered hair;
Have her chef prepare
A banquet for all the heads of state:
Let them advance between the Spartan guards,
And past the priest and past the poet.
Let the music play, have them dance,
And rocking in your rocking chair,
Point to a state of possibility:
The fragile arts of peace
Shatter the weather of war.

Now six gray horses draw you to where you are,
Not to Versailles, Sparta, or Athens.
The seventh horse is wild and black
And riderless and paws the streets of Washington
Where you are rocking and will always rock.

John Fitzgerald Kennedy,
You could not stop the shells,
The drowning of your boat in war;
You could not stop the snow the sky dumped down,
The cold, the lectern smoking when your priest invoked
The Lord, your poet struck blind, the bullets in your head,
The six gray horses drawing you to where you are
Rocking and will always rock.

The seventh horse is riderless, wild and black.

I M J F K

We may stop worrying.
Our best man died.
We know of no one now we can not spare.

Our man was *BADLY* shot.
The marksman hit the mark:
a straightshooter.
                    Still

The trigger was not triggered by a thought
nor by the shooting pain of high ideals
but purifying faith's anathema.

Our man was shot.
From a blind. In a blind flash of error.
By a blind thug.

He hit the bullseye.
And he never knew
the center of our circle was unique.

How to find words for the depriver
            You should not have done that brother enemy?
            You painted our forehead with your mark?
                    (the fighter can not see Athene)

Our man now rests where bone pale crosses bloom
among well ordered rows of bloody plantings
moist from the sorry dew of love

ROY FULLER

FROM A FOREIGN LAND

Sceptical of the cult, suspicious of the nation,
Nevertheless we had to grant the amelioration
Of the one by the other; and certainly the alternative
Had seemed of depressing threat.

Given this tepid and grudging view, why do we yet
Flinch from the murdered consul's images, remember
(In the far February following the November)
That the spouse still has to live?

It's not that by their taste for intellect disarmed
We were unconsciously adherents all the time,
Nor that strong vulnerable youth unfairly charmed,
But that the senseless crime

Is what for us he had the power to postpone
Who now approach within the assassin's range alone.

JAMES L. WEIL

A KIND OF LIBATION
for J. F. K.

Sorry I
can't pour with

my manners
manhood my

unsteady
ness spilling.

J E R O M E   G .   R O T H E N B E R G

CORTÈGE

The drums have entered my heart;
The creak of caisson over unprepared
Terrain; the tight clop of the slowed hooves;
The swaying. We have at last met,
Sealed from harm's reach, having ridden earlier
Different ways. It is late, and I ask
Whether riding with you now
Will make a difference.
Is it enough to live that beat
One mile or three, to climb the hill
That watches Lincoln, to wait,
Wait for love to catch up?
We are stretched together; I do not
See the avenue, the avenue is only where my blood
Points, the rumble is within, the procession
Is breath, breath, breath, breath.
I feel a river below; the hooves are hollow;
We pass, suspended: the dead breath,
The breathing dead. Now the grave.
Darkness is a book, a friend.
I wait your signal.
When is the earth, still loosely packed,
Ready for me to rise?
The way back is dense, but clear.
You have returned with me.

A DEATH BEFORE KILLING

Raw ulcers and his aspirin signify
Love lost and loose as a cannon splintering
A hull, as, decks awash, and foundering,
He staggers up the sheer of a wave as high
As childhood's surge to shores he never reached.
And he hungers for a speech that might unsay
The flesh marooned, the ghost forever beached
On a small uncharted island of dismay.

Round him shoal waters heave and crash.
Birdflights cut hieroglyphs in a sky
He may not read. At night reefs gnash
And rip the bottoms out of dreams, and the Dry
Tortuga of his day drains all his leaf
As the sail, forgiveness, shrinks to a handkerchief.

H. L. MOUNTZOURES

THREE NIGHTS OF MOURNING: JOHN F. KENNEDY

I. The Night of the Murder

The sea begins, far out beyond the light,
His stalk in iron boots,
Spitting foam, slobbering shells of teeth,
Green-black rage spinning from his eyes—
Advances, nearly swoons, begins to run,
Arches, screams, pounds upon his victim's throat—
Long, white, exposed and soft, blood beating
Blue within:

> Asleep, stretched out with veins torn,
> Sandy mouth murmuring Forgive,
> Sandy hair washing in the bloodhungry
> Arms of his perverted lover.

And run, my heart says, watching.
No one walks on water here.
No salvation, loaves of wondrous feeding,
No nets of splendid fishes. Only the victim
And the cold discarded spear.

II. The Night of the Burial

The light flashes, two whites, one red,
In pulsing affirmation of our cycle's
Real stability.
And the sea walks slowly, calm,
Taking the air at twilight time.
He wears white spats, green corduroy,
Holds a dapper violet umbrella.
He mumbles absently about his dotage,

Although the fun's at hand of courting sky,
Breeze, and all the lovely swarming elements.
For somehow as he wanders, murmuring,
He seems to see as in a liquid dream
The fact of his antiquity:
Is he not a shriveled king sitting on a throne
Beneath a million tons of swirling conscience,
Conscience eddying through magnesium
Jagged holes that were his eyes and mouth,
And, stone-struck, does he not hear with awe
. Innocent fishes whispering through the socket
Of his heart:
        You killed your son, you mauled
        The child, then threw the sword
        Upon the silver sand.
But no. He is a dandy prince meandering.
He steps lightly, meets one of his girls
Wreathed in cloud, periwinkle earrings, sunset eyes:
He sibilates her long white throat with jeweled hand.

I am not afraid.
The sun sinks in melded rage.
A single star memorizes
All the bitter glory of this day.
I wonder at the calmness of the sea.

III. A Night One Month After

The sea is brave.
He wears no coat, no boots
This stinging night of wind and sleet.
He holds his curly head up high defiantly,
His white teeth exposed in perfect laughter.
The vast hole of his mouth is rinsed
With whisky incense of the sky.
He knows he cannot die.
He has forgotten death and what a murder

Is or may become. His brawny hands caress
Skeletons of ships dangling on the rocks:
He plucks a broken mast and uses it
To pick his teeth.
His business goes on. He is full
Of holy passion: rising, puff,
Glutting on the moon's horn of sensual time
And falling, empty, on her whim.
Whether he crushes, wild, or dances, proud,
Or merely cowers in drunk at three o'clock
To the dinging lullaby of buoy—is told
And unimportant now. He sleeps.
He is majesty. He must arise tomorrow,
Feel the bottom of his bed to find what bone
To no avail tried to irritate his sleep,
His long alluvial dream.

I neither run away nor acquiesce.
I stand and button up my thick black coat
Against the wind and hail and try hard not to cry.
Tonight I wish to feel my own self-pity,
To mourn the profane technic of this life.
But I see the sea lurch,
Cry out and die, then come once more alive
(Murderer and murdered, concomitant),
Always attempting conversation with the living;
I know the crush of all of us
Beneath our floating salt indifferent death,
And what is my small sorrow,
What grain of sand abrading,
Moving in mercy at the mercy
Of a power not mine nor yet its own?

TRACTION

His brother said that pain was what he knew.
Pain's wit is irony. It took two
Bullets to bring that straight back down. They said
One bullet had exploded in his head.

The unforeseen becomes inevitable.
Who would have thought, on that bloody day,
That back that had survived the terrible
Would take the head down with it all the way?

We saw another back. It killed the killer,
Who had killed twice. Three murders done,
The one before our eyes like a cheap thriller
Run and re-run. That week-end of the gun,

Twenty-one salutes, his epitaph,
Back-fired on a billion screens at noon.
We loved his luck until it broke in half.
The end comes back. It always comes too soon.

RICHARD FROST

ON NOT WRITING AN ELEGY

My friend told me about kids in a coffee house
who laughed and celebrated the killing. Another friend
didn't care, sick at his own divorce,
drinking martinis with a delicate hand,
saying he couldn't care when I said I cried
like everybody. Still, I am the vain one,
a bullet in my shoulder, six seconds to go
before another burns in my head. Trying
to write about the thing, I always end
by feeling I have been shot. My brain, my spine
gone, and with time winding foolishly,
I am raced, tabled, cleaned out, boxed, flown,
carried and lowered in. I have had this done
on a shiny day with my wife and bodyguards
and everyone there to cry out, and I have cried
without trying and without a clear thought.
This death has had me where I cannot write
or hate or love, numb as a coined face
fallen where all flames have only to burn
down. Lost where I must only lose my place,
I mourn the glories of our blood and state.

MARJORIE MIR

FOUR DAYS IN NOVEMBER

In late autumn sun
This coldness without season.
Strangers asking how.

A long rain today,
Cold against the face, has quenched
Final disbelief.

No movement of hours
Disturbs this room or betrays
The sly leap of pain.

Once restless as wind,
His quickness borne in slow march.
Nothing in its time.

DONALD L. JONES

NOVEMBER 22, 1963

There the guard changes,
the Soldier stays
abstract and stiff
within his tomb.

Here in Nebraska
the wind bursts
over the bare space
of the nation's heart—

our son and father
Known but turned to flame
against the vast affront
we bear time out of mind.

MARVIN SOLOMON

THE ASSASSINATION
November 22, 1963

Muzak played its groceries;
The goaded shopping-carts approached the check-outs
To the tune of cash. By these,
The wives and husbands were excused
Into the night, where it was happening.

A cold wind swarmed the parking-lots
To snatch the babes from arms,
And foil ignition keys in locks.
Newspapers flew in anguished shapes of sunken boats
And crashed airplanes, that mocked

The weekend glut. "My God!"
They thought, as all the shops blew dark,
"When will it stop!" But stars' gunpowders splayed out
Cycles from that fatal shot,
Doors slammed, glass shattered

At the shock. White and taut,
In prairies of arc-light, they stood,
Embracing packages of emptiness they bought.
"But surely everything will be all right!"
They said, and thought of children

Home. Triggered by calamities,
They scattered in their cars like ricochets.
The nitred dust descended in the supermarts on buys
They hadn't thought to risk—on flesh
Gone slack with wounds,

Pale lip and dilate eye in freeze
Of impact with that regulated cold

That steadies, row on row, the memories
Of living lips and living eyes.
Found wanting, all green leafage

Of the field, fruit plucked
In ripeness fallowing to worm,
And sweet elixers guaranteed to slake
Whatever thirst. In vacuum packs,
Vacuum; in bottles, cartons, cans,

Time and all its hopeful nutrients
Were stacked. Rummaging hunger
Found them stale or fraudulent or of prohibitive
            expense.
Just after noon, the sudden mark-downs
Moved the customers, but not

The stock. And lilacs bloomed
Again in dooryards where no prices were,
In nickel-cold November, for that prime
Cut down, that valor dimmed, mid-gleam,
That strength and bravery that dared

Against the deadly marksmanship
Of fame, and so were killed.
Who could afford that blood?—or stop
Its endless bartering gone cheap?
Opened up at nine,

Next day the markets sold him—
Body, pride, and aura—like a bargain-day.
Tills coffined mourners for so many books of stamps;
And ketchups, toilet tissues, instant coffees loomed
Like heroes, through giveaways of tears.

SONNET FOR JOHN-JOHN

My father died in nineteen thirty-four,
When I was ten. It too was sudden; while
He turned in bed, a blood clot touched his heart.
Not bullets, but an old wound of the world
Unhealed, surprised him dead. And relatives
Ate heavy meals, and cried, and ate and cried
Again. Remembering but token love—
And most, hot temper, heavy beatings—I
Was quiet, and enjoyed my cousins. I
Must tell you this, somehow, because of wounds
That never heal. Our fathers die and die
Again in aching graves of withheld words
    They did not say. While we re-live the pain
    Of severance from the sons we might have been.

RICHARD EBERHART

THE KILLER

On the Assassination of President Kennedy

There I go, with an inscrutable face,
Controlled by the gunsight of hate.
My own accuser, raging with despair,
I kill the clean American air.

All dreams of love are dim.
I kill myself in killing him.
I am of Satan, the expression
Of evil will through my aggression.

I do not know what I do.
Vileness is deep, is ever new.
My fate is to have been sent
To kill my own friend and President.

I do not know what I do.
Love left me. No love was true.
I did not know I sealed my fate
In denying love to love but hate.

Hate woke hate. My savage fashion
Begot an equally savage passion.
The bullet that shocked a nation
Came back to bring my own annihilation,

Came back in such Satanic style
Justice is denied my trial.
I reduced to savagery
Those who could have made my spirit free.

THE SPIRIT OF
POETRY SPEAKS

Each man must suffer his fate,
Whether it comes by love, or by hate.
Kennedy lies in Arlington,
Who loved mankind, who strove for peace.
The killer has no redemption,
Shuffled into his grave by the police.
None can escape the crack of doom.
Alone, all come to a narrow room.

NOVEMBER 22, 1963

It was, they say, the left hand struck him down.
It does not matter which extreme.
All men, to murder, strike from the edge
of the same great gulf into which
they see themselves falling, endlessly.
This political plane on which we mark
the arrows, right and left, has no edges
from which extremists fall,
far from each other's sight.
More like a ball, our situation seems,
partaking of the enigma of the circle, the fearful,
boundless, sphere. There, moving out to east
or west, repelled from one-another,
taking the way you now feel best,
you can go full circle—but you may,
on the midpoint, on the obverse, dark meridian,
meet, as in a mirror, marred and flaked,
the face of him from whom you fled in hate.
Smash his image and you break
your own in a hundred shining, silver pieces,
sharp as knives to let the blood of husbands,
children, fathers, wives—whose love you need not have,
but only share. Still I would not have,
even for this, half a world.
Some must risk, must chart the dark side, mark
the mirrors and mirages so, slowly,
we may learn to go—anywhere, to any man,
to circumnavigate this fearsome sphere with love.

JOHN TAGLIABUE

THE YOUNG PRESIDENT: MARCH 1964

He sort
of embodied
the air he sort
of embodied the
air where democracy
stood tall, Jefferson
and Robert Frost were
his advisors, he sort
of clearly gave evidence of
wit and democracy and me
and you and humor, Irish,
American, young, and bright, the
air when it is windy and strong and
clear, our love when it is bright and clear,
our children when they are tall and bright,
he standing in the wind does call to him
    gallant summarizers of democracies' tunes
    and like an unbreakable enlightening
    Musician standing on the sea spray
    he says with that young courage
    Wake up to Humanity's love,
    precise politician of such
    steadfast shaking
    Luminosity.

WALTER KAUFMANN

THE FALL
November 22, 1963

We fall like leaves
that drowse and drop,
and any grief
that outlives winter
drowns in the heedless
floods of spring.

Few fall like oaks,
breaking the branches
of some that stood near,
leaving a space
that many a summer
fails to fill.

Your fall,
like Agamemnon's,
shook the earth;
beyond the seas
strange women wailed
in empty terror.

Like Agamemnon,
you were a man
until you fell—
power and faults
more than replaceable.
Then, all at once,

your fall was hardly
some man's whom fate
had briefly raised,

one who survived
an endless war
and now leaves orphans:

Agamemnon dead
was not that king,
no, not the man
Achilles loathed,
sacker of cities
treading purple robes,

one who conceivably
deserved to die—
as who does not?—
and fated anyway:
as if a few
years mattered.

Pity is dwarfed by terror:
leaves we behold
as through a glass,
wistful and distant,
and even the oak
is a stranger.

Your fall crashed the glass:
though the seasons
change on the stage,
torrents of spring
cannot still the icy
wind from outside.

That men will speak
endlessly as of
Atreus' son
of you, too,

seems less than this breach
you struck unknowing,

struck unconscious.
Shivering,
we feel the blindness
even of princes
whose fame is so unlike
all they imagined.

Your growth is beggared
by the splintering crash.
But had you done less,
you might have fallen,
a floating leaf
that drops to sleep.

FOR JOHN KENNEDY, JR.

Stand at attention
for a moment
lit as birthday candle
or bullet

This is your father
and our brother
in outer space
weather

Be straight with
your man's
eye on dark
providence

Grow. You have a flag
and scrap
of black
crepe

ALAN ANSEN

THE DEATH OF NEARCHUS

A Threnody in the Form of a Pastoral Dialogue

In memoriam J.F.K. 1917–1963

Melampsus.   This death is timely.

Mopsus.   Most untimely. There on the heights of life
Looks and manner gave a momentary unfamiliar
Grace to power, power that brownly sticks
In the throats and the ways of the arithmetical mass.

Melampsus.   A cipher can vote No
With his trigger finger
Against the insolence
Of pretensions to charm and good will
On the part of the already gifted
With what ought to make charm and good will
Unnecessary.

Mopsus.   On the contrary. Every act of force supplicates
Some countervailing smile, some interceding dance
         to deny
What the devil and gravity inculcate all too
         intimately,
That what can be measured is altogether joyless.

Melampsus.   Let us keep that illusion.
The fear of the assassin
Is wholesome for nymphs and demigods;
And the hope of the assassin,
Balm to a troglodyte folk.

98

Mopsus.   Nearchus and Nearcha were not flouting
             The shiftless and inexpedient submerged
             But quickening their brutish lymph
             With shows of featness, with aspiring sounds,
             To share with their leaders an ungrudging delight
             In all excellence in the manifold of fields
             American hospitality unfences for talents.

Melampsus.   And that anarch generosity
                Rewards the untalented too
                With a liberal target
                For their discontents.
                And among the discontented papers vented,
                Was a cartridge.

Mopsus.   So new to state, so eager in their child-bearing,
             Their feelings toward one another and the world,
             The play of mind and feature that united them
             And them to what quickens, what grows
                          and exfoliates in life
             Blanked by the spurt and drip of ever more
                          meaningless blood!
             The tears of an ungrateful people require
             An adequate inadequacy for this high negation's agent.

Melampsus.   Sir, he lacked advancement.

99

CHANNEL U.S.A.—LIVE

We all were passengers in that motorcade,
caught in the dust of a far street
and the stars of flags blown, as the car moved,
bubble-top down, brown hair tossed
above a face familiar as our own.

At home in easy chairs, turning a dial
to bring the image close—the smile, the wave,
the harps of motorcycles and of cheers—
we were, in spite of miles or parties, there;
and ride there still, the underpass ahead,
a building's shadow falling like a tomb
across the narrowing street, the dust, this room
in California-Iowa-Maine,
                              the rifle ready, aimed.

Most screens are black and white,
and blood seems only a darker stain.
The carpet's pastel color stays the same,
sofas unblotched. But one fabric turned red
where his torn head had lain.

He campaigned on crutches once;
once scratched a message on a savage coast,
swam more than once through pain,
rescued lost comrades, fought the foam
of inactivity in high, white beds,
worked toward action, wrote,
replaced a brother whom we never knew,
climbed up from foreign fields and died at home
in a loud street where a rifle leaned
its long, blue beak,
                              ready and aimed

A wreath lies where the bullet stopped.
A continent beyond, a live torch burns,
and we, by limousine and plane and jeep,
ride in the flickering caravan,
still caught on an unsteady screen
where westerns blast and haunt our sleep,
making each day the long commute
out of the muck of every street
toward a reviving flame.

We all were passengers, and are,
driving and driven through the sweep
of shadows, sunlight, flags, and love—
but one of us stood up and faced
                    the rifle that is always aimed,
and left the image that we keep.

GEORGE T. WRIGHT

FOR A WEDDING PERFORMED ON THANKSGIVING IN THE WEEK OF PRESIDENT KENNEDY'S DEATH

The sunny day, the mild cool,
Love in the air, thinking a rhyme,
The smiles of industry and school,
All argue this an easy time.
But in the stages of the old,
Grandmothers, elders, gray, divorced,
In bachelor, groom, father, cold
Gladnesses, hardly the last.
Moving into the wooden rows,
Passive while the organ pumps,
We know of light beyond the windows,
But heavy now the triumph thumps.
We breathe together a little while
Attendant on the groom and bride.
After the service, down the aisle
Family, friends, guests re-divide.
O yet when order tears apart,
When loosening murder wakes and ages,
We have to beat it still with art:
Repeated sounds and bordered stages.
We must be thankful just to find
A structure here, a symbol there,
And know, as in this couple signed,
Whatever hope we have we share.

WE WHO DO NOT GRIEVE
IN SILENCE

1

First came the special issues of the magazines
With loyal photographs: the old rich times, the rocking chair,
The wife who knew who Dali is, the muscular war,
The politics retouched and smiling, the happy hammer
Of his power, the idiocy of death. Fifty cents.

The president was dead, tears fell and incomes rose.
      Wait, brothers, wait,
      My grief has gone to market too.

2

The picture books cost more but they were meant to last,
They used the most caressing words, like strong ideals
And dedicated heart and faith in our democracy.
And those who sold the plaster statuettes (one dollar each),
Their right hand mourned, their left rang up the cash.

The president was dead, laments and incomes rose.
      Wait, brothers, wait,
      My grief has gone to market too.

3

Congressmen deplored into the cameras, the voters saw
Their simple, manly sorrow. Foreign crowns were caught
Bowing usefully toward the poor man's grave.
All were shocked; what's more, they really were; alas
One could not keep one's honest sobs untelevized.

103

The president was dead, tears fell and reputations rose;
>Wait, brothers, wait,
>>My grief has gone to market too.

4

Next came the records, and his voice was heard again
To make flesh creep from shore to shore. A publisher
Withdrew a luckless exposé; a sensitive biography
Recouped the loss. Three journalists retold the terror
Irreversible. We shuddered, covered up our eyes, and bought.

The president was dead, laments and incomes rose.
>Wait, brothers, wait,
>>My grief has gone to market too.

5

When great men breathe their last, their expiration
Swells our sails. Films shall be turned, sermons released,
Memoirs composed and statues erected. Pure grief is silent, yes,
And yet pure hardness is too hard for us as well. We are
Our comedy: the standards we betray, we made.

The president is dead; my poem goes to press;
>Grief, brothers, grief
>>Is my profit, but all the same I grieve.

104

VERBA IN MEMORIAM

How to speak of it
when words today go
rapidly downhill to hide
under the grasses,

To let the stanza
on its miraculous wheels
convey
what was man
and existed as the warm road
we still ride
and run after.

Deciding, after all, it is the land
that goes on expanding,
contracting, a place
that is green
or sandy, that is marsh
or mountain
very like words.

I am going to use
these words
they were always usable
and useful to this man.

He would not object
to phrases
hiding themselves
under the grasses

He has found them there.

The earth is now
more constant
to him
than are we who need
the upper air.

What he had planned
had something of the classic in it
i.e. to say he thought
in marble

We understood
despite those turns
of elegiac
that he wished

Where he lived
where he *once* lived
to be consecrated
to *Demos*

Despite his welcome
to princes
his reading of their scrolls.

This was youthful
and proper
for one who desired
an heroic name

To be inscribed
on his tomb
and so it was.

But the inscription
must include
our names

106

Who lived in his time.

Who now can be said
to be a lonely
generation

As if one more
of our artists
had died

And there were only
a few
who remained

Admiring the columns
the temple still standing
the grasses
fresh as a cupful
of light

The way
a new word strikes
the tender skin.

DAVID RAY

ON SEEING A MOVIE BASED ON AN EPISODE FROM PRESIDENT KENNEDY'S LIFE

Tonight we took
the boys to see
PT Boat 1
09 at the
Dryden Drive-In
3 boys in the
Volkswagen and
our daughter of
course. Before that
we had to watch
Bob Mitchum chase
a tiger with
a torch and then
like Wilson in
Hemingstein's best
story steal the
girl indifferent
ly. Jack Hawkins
tried to shoot him
too. The boys said
this was scary.
In the next car
a man shoved his
girl down in the
seat and had at
her, I turned the
mirror and watched
his shirt going
up and down, it
took about eight

or ten minutes.
I think it was
their first time, they
lit cigarettes
then Jack, dead Jack
came on and we
saw him choose his
PT boat, fix
er up and head
for battle. Av-
rom had to pee
just then and wd-
nt go outside
on the gravel
so we had to
leave. I loved Jack
Kennedy, he
wanted better
for us than these
Drive-in thumpings.
Under the great
stars of Amer-
ica there should
be better, we
were choked on car
fumes, to go down
town wd be worse.
On the way home
we passed trailer
parks, the sad young
marrieds inside
watching T.V.
Why shouldn't they
give up and hug
if they can't walk
out into the

night without get-
ting gassed? They know
their dreams are put
to sleep like pups.

W. H. AUDEN

ELEGY FOR J. F. K.

Why *then?* Why *there?*
Why *thus,* we cry, did he die?
The Heavens are silent.

What he was, he was:
What he is fated to become
Depends on us.

Remembering his death,
How we choose to live
Will decide its meaning.

When a just man dies,
Lamentation and praise,
Sorrow and joy are one.

EDWARD POLS

FOR JOHN KENNEDY
OF HARVARD

A tumult of images insist,
Repeat, repeat, traverse, and re-traverse,
Until the dreadful Sunday's counterpoint—
She with your children pacing to the drum,
While here the prisoner comes, and dies
Under the blind resurge of violent Dallas—
Is on the night screen one more time rehearsed
And we believe at last
What on the Friday we so feared to know.

That Friday night St. Patrick's bells
Came to me in an old Maine house
The while against them spoke—spoke
The banal words each of us finds when moved
And when a public voice exacts reply—
Spoke the various accents of the city.
Some nuance unmanned me yet again
(Or was it the passing of my youth that struck?)
So, lest the children see my tears,
I walked awhile between the arbor and the barn
And thought of you passing once in 'thirty-seven
In the spring of freshman year and of your life
On the Yard walk past Widener's steps and
Up the slope towards Palmer House that was:
There stood a Norway maple on that hill
Which every spring spread out a cope
Of greeny gold upon the ground, and there we passed,
Treading the bright minuscule blossom down,
In the slant light of morning and of our lives.

Your smile held then—how shall I say?—a thought
Too much assurance, and your walk a pride

To daunt a green and envious boy who'd wrought
A manner but no ease for all he tried
To be at home: you seemed to own the place
I loved but did not yet possess. But stay,
There comes to mind the man of forty-five:
A man who wore that humor in his face
Did not let youth or wealth or rank betray
Him to forget this truth: when we arrive
Who come here late, the place we meant to find
And win and love is altered out of mind.

So, much of worth in what we take is lost—
That Harvard gone of Eliot and of James,
That land of Arcady before the host
Of yours and mine sailed here to stake their claims.
Provincial places though (your smile confides)
And not perhaps as open to the world
As we with myriad ties of blood and faith
Have made them in your time; and this abides,
For all the poise that's vanished with your wraith,
For all that Camelot's banners need be furled:
They changed to take us in, but we
Transformed them out of all they could foresee.

The tree is gone that once bestrewed the ground
Each springtime with a green-gold grace:
Now buildings flank that place,
While, moved and turned around,
Cropped Palmer House looks strange—
So all things shift and change—
But though your life is gone and my youth
I see you now in truth
Transfigured, resplendent in our ruth.
They say you were still half symbol,
Being given so little time;
Come, let us take you so, but in this sense:
In that region of possibility you fill

There, still, your bright incontinent essence
Inclines to its own completion, still
Shapes almost its own actuality, still contrives
Some reason, measure, humor in our lives.

GREGORY CORSO

LINES WRITTEN
NOV. 22, 23—1963
— in Discord —

So what's it like being an American Assassin
                              this silly uncertain day?

Not I with chiromancerian eyes
   Do I raise my right hand that Popes halt
   Talmudians relent?
Like a table of fishy Chinamen
   I laugh my purpose into dopey disguise
Who'll see this
   or that
   or where-they're-at
bereft of such eyes?

         The Good   The Bad
         I seek the Good
         But *I Am* Good!
         Thus the bad, O damn, O thank God, I'm sure to find.

Heed me all you creepy goopy assassins!
         I am a million jinns! I build ins and outs and ins!
I'm all them gremlins! dropping wrenches
         in BOAC'S BOEINGS
         . . . sticking pins in zeppelins!
O I am a zillion million stars twinkling in the all crazy fars!
I am innumerable illuminable sins!
         I am indoomable ingloomable
And the uncreation of the world is the work of every
         humanable human imaginable!
         —all are assassins!
And I swear to you are Indians less cruel no I swear to you

115

hashish has never been your gruel
you drunken inexorbitant square killer non-hashadins!
One poke of red-eyed hash would make all of you hail it iatrical
not homicidal not rifle not Presidental
Aye you are punk killers not assassins!

Ah, the Disney dinosaur's light laughter
& a little blonde girl's tears
What sad what sick what damned juxtaposition!
monster and child, punk and President
society and poet, bullets and flesh
Bullets the size of Coney Island fishing worms
can obliterate blix pow-out the whole shebang
No man's the whole bit
But that young President was more than a little bit
The captain should go down when his ship goes down
But when the captain dies . . . the ship sails on—
O failure Christ

Come you illiterate creepy dumbbells harken the cry
of the *true* Assassin!
I damn! I hail!
I summon the Blessed Lord of the Ice Cold Nanook Country
and eat raw seal meat with Him!
I curse the earth in Space and in Time!
I pee upon the Evolution of the Rocks!
I weep upon the first living things!
Bang my fists on the unknown age of the world!
I vomit up Natural Selection and the Change of the Species!
I augh like a sick dinosaur o'er
the invasion of the dry lands by Life!
I smirk at the butterfly like a pimply-faced stumble-bum!
By the wings I yank by the wings the wings the lovely wings
By the throat I smote the Age of the Reptile!
So too the Age of the Mammal!
So too O very much so the Ancestry of Man!

116

Man descended from a walking ape!
I awake the lazy greasy Neanderthal and spit in his
                                    big sad stupid eye!
I pummel my Colt .38 into the iron skin of the
                                    Palaeolithic muralist!
I look contemptuously down upon the screwed-up
                                    Neolithic creep!
I beckon the coming of those early bastards much like
        ourselves today and blow a sadistic breath of death
        in their hoary faces!

        O orange owls! O ambitious green!
I sneak upon the beginning of earth's cultivation
        and sow poisoned polly-seeds
        ahead of the prehistoric farmer's burning reap
I am there at the flooding of the Mediterranean Valley
        and watch the thousand life drown and die!
I enter the earliest thought, the most primitive philosophy,
        and drive mad dreams and sick fears into the Old Man,
        the Priest, the Vestal
I turn the stars and seasons into giant hideous creatures!
I inject the word cancer the word kill the word hate into the
        Aryan tongue
        the Semitic tongue
        the Hamitic Ural-Altaic and Chink tongues!
I am there watching the earliest nomads stop to build Ur, Sumer
I shall strike a flashlight into the Sumerians' eyes
                                    and mystify them nuts!
I have poisoned Sargon! Stabbed Hammurabi!
        Like the Pest I wiped out the Assyrians!
        the Chaldeans!
I grabbed the history of ancient Egypt and India and China
        and infested it with the big lie of Bel-Marduk
        and God-Kings
        and ordered Shi Hwang-ti, like a dowser a goat,
        to destroy all records!

117

I have made goats of every King every Pope every puny
        clubbed-foot Elect
        in every chapter of that history I puke up like bile
        . . . like bile

        Now the Rains of Darkness begin
The entire stellified crop   out!
Sags the wick like a limp giraffe neck   like a sick nose
And lo! on the back of a wet firefly
        comes Hi-Fi
        yet mournful   yet I am the one to suffer
        whose thousand years attempt at being
                the Great Assassinator
        has failed to dump even Methuselah

        O brown fortune! I shake your devils!
So small am I to the proportion of so small a tree
And a sun so small in that sunny sea called Eternity
Insignificant sun! Lamp of lard! Bright ant faked God!
        Conjurer of string beans!
O so small am I   and smaller the things I eat and believe
        O tiny Adam O shrimp Eve
So it is   So it shall come to be
The gap caused by my magnified midgetry shall become
        someday like all great China
        the China basin for the new China sea!
And so Kennedy   and so America
        and so A and so B and so C
With a full arrow and ½ bow   I'll lay em low

        O Lord of Ducks! O Fame of Death!
        When a captain dies
        The ship doesn't sink
        And though the crew weeps the loss
        The stars in the skies
        are still boss.

118

KENNEDY POEM

The shot, the horse
snaps open in the sky,

the parts drift slowly
down, the caliph

with them, red
& white, an arrow

in his head, into the gaps
between pink domes,

someone else with a girl
drifts by on a carpet;

i went to bed with ice cream
now i go angrily

& will not sleep;
murder stretches

as far as i remember;
here is another gift

for the barbed wire
of our heads, tho

voices now have a brief
tenderness requiring

panoply, soldiers, horses,
drums, & an astonishing

119

emptiness love denied;
"stunned" & meant

just that, with something
less official which

possibly remains:
pope & holy man

on a mountain,
bare trees, birds,

sick, lame, stupid, dead
listening avidly to

nothing new but to which
nothing is alien,

a waterfall briefly
clean for belief,

tho now we are watching
the fights again.

120

CAROL BERGÉ

PAVANE FOR THE
WHITE QUEEN

The Loved Wife Falling Slowly Awake

for JBK

I. In the Rooms of Music

Not as the word death. But
as confusion: memory of bells
into voices of broken bells,
sound of torn strings: songs
into this silent scream. Not
the keening of the loveless,
the ugly in their disarrayed
skins. Who have not tasted
rooms of music shaped as eyes
through flesh: woman near man.
Not as the word death. But
as samisen gone suddenly mute,
shut memory of night voices
into sharp shriek: crackling,
as when eyes shatter. I move
toward your empty room. Begin
stopping the usual gestures.
To cease listening. The sound
of music in eye-shaped rooms
having stopped with one note.

II. In the Street of Eyes

Eventually, it happens. I move
into our streets, slowly. I see
his head; its shape is almost yours.
He is not you. At first I thought.

121

Or that man. Or that. A tall man
near the door. In that car. The
park yesterday. Shops. It is a
slow nightmare of wrong faces, turn
of cheek, memory of your jawline,
eyes, the way your feet would
strike the pavement and pivot you.
Shadows of occasional hell, as
someone unconsciously imitates you.
I am supposed to know where you are,
that no city contains you whole.
Yet this odd stumbling over raw or
stunning hints: this looking into
the sudden stranger's unloved face!

III. In the Dust House

This furniture which was ours
talks clumsily about our loving.
I thought we were bound by wood,
leather, cloth of our own skins:
now my thinner dark skull stops
before reaching our silk pillows.
How to move, to sleep, now that
your warm skull has become stone!
where marble dust congeals to
walls, rooms down which my feet
run noiselessly and motionless
in thick night or sharp dreams
cushioning one shrill red day:
God! that your feet are gone!
and mine, marking out the hours,
perform a mockery of minuets
amid the velvet and the marble.
Candles, sunlight that glinted
when your eyes shaped our days
turn now to flares of anguish,

122

all flames go dull, the magic
slips through my fingers, marks
blood on parquet, on old satin,
the mourners note my vertebrae
impressed into my white cape.
It was this castle we once lit,
our lives parallel to love, to
deep sleep, gentle confidences.
With the same cry as that child
who bears your eyes, I am turned
toward the watchers, in their
terrible distance of armchairs,
of pages: my cheeks and ribs
blanched, immolated beneath a
careful avalanche of pale powder
and papers: and am remembering
our hands, our feet, as it was
when we moved unaware in rooms
of careless laughter, banquets,
beds warm into a sleep of love
where you have gone without me.
The sounds, the rooms fragment
and drift, it is too quiet, the
love having stopped with you,
the castle flakes like paint,
I become my own skin and turn
before their eyes into marble
lit from within by your face,
voice stilled by one red note.

ANTHONY OSTROFF

INTIMATE PARTY IN GUADALAJARA, DEC. 1963

Jorge Hernandez, architect,
Said, "Culture's bad enough
Elsewhere. In Mexico it's worse."
Things are tough,
              I thought
All over. Said, "That's the curse
Of the modern world." Did Jorge add, "Except
Architecture." (Cough) "And a little art?"
Mas o menos. Give or take
                    a few.
He left Rivera out, put
Orozco and Siqueiros in.
An uncompromising Catholic.
"We have the Mayas, Aztecs, take your pick.
—But understand, we're not like you."
A long tradition.
                "Then came Spain
And learned the stone at hand."
His lovely wife, at hand,
Said not a word, but smiled
Whenever Jorge spoke. Such absurd
Love! Love as if the world
Were neither *mas o menos.*
                          O
The young elite of Mexico
Afford their love their beauty!
So I turned: "Señor Diaz," I said,
"Forgive my French. *Que tal?*"
That handsome young man's smile,
                              bred
By friendship more than aristocracy,

124

Gave upon *his* wife
                who understood
A little English, too. (O what's to do?
We're all too early and too late.)
We could not speak Spanish. They
Could not speak English,
                        save
Señor Diaz, who nobly faced his fate:
"Translate!" his soul commanded.
I served more drinks.
                        "What do you think
Of Kennedy?"
                The room
Designed by Jorge, spun
And swelled, contracted. "SOME
MADMAN
                Madman
                        madman . . ."
"God!" my wife burst out.
"We think it was a plot!" Jorge announced.
"Too much coincidence."
"*In the United States*," I pronounced,
"We believe in madmen
                        and incompetence."
A plot, a plot
                aplotaplotaplot
"Your history is full of plots." (my wife
Serenely) "Ours is not."
Her eyes, aglisten, stopped them short.
"We understand. We sympathize.
He was a great, a very great man."
"*Si! Si!*" A nodding of heads.
Jorge's black hair, the tall hairdos
Of the two lovely wives
Accorded us Señor Diaz.
And architecture. Add

125

The pure, sweet love
Of those two wives
Attending sorrow
Silently,
Their untranslatable smiles
Translated:
"Si.
    Si."

DOWN IN DALLAS

Down in Dallas, down in Dallas
Where the shadow of blood lies black
Lee Oswald nailed Jack Kennedy up
With the nail of a rifle crack.

The big bright Cadillacs stomped on their brakes
And the man in the street fell still
When the slithering gun like a tooth of sin
Coiled back from the window sill.

In a white chrome room on a table top,
Oh, they tried all a scalpel knows
But they couldn't spell stop to that drop-by-drop
Till it bloomed to a rigid rose.

Down on the altar, down on the altar
Christ blossoms in bread and wine
But each asphalt stone where the blood dropped down
Is burst to a cactus spine.

Oh down in Dallas, down in Dallas
Where a desert wind walks by night
Lee Oswald nailed Jack Kennedy up
On the cross of a rifle sight.

ROBERT G. TUCKER

A MEMORIAL FOR PRESIDENT KENNEDY

The old man's fleet that wounded the Pacific
Flew all the flags half-mast, but we were young.
Despite the wound, in that war you saved lives;
Such was the deed to live by, and you lived,
Bringing a healthy radiance to sick times.
But short and cheap in Dallas he held life
Who caused the flags sink half-way down again,
And young no more, we can not have you old.

Such as you were, so would a man become:
Despite the night, the risk, the wound, to dare
Stay true and, out of savage war, save life;
Then, healing cold war scars, your hand stretched forth
An agency disarming, a corps of peace,
A ban to tests of madness down the sky;
In Dallas you had mind of Birmingham.
It sought true cures for prejudice, your heart.

Not short nor cheap you held life, teaching how
All schisms mend as we will sacrifice
Our human selves, accept wounds, for a world
Where no life's short nor cheap, but held in love.
We will not have you old. And young no more,
We give ourselves outright, as you have done,
To nothing less—mind, hand, and heart—than man.
And may the God who made us bind this true.

128

LOUIS ZUKOFSKY

FINALLY A VALENTINE

There is
a heart

has no
complaint

better a-
part

than
faint

so the
faintest

part of
it

has no
complaint—

a
part.

BY THIS TO REMEMBER

By this to remember, this spring again
As we walk by the river, the tidal Charles,
And the golden dome of the Statehouse glints
In the sun, and the cars on Storrow Drive
Glitter, rushing chrome suns before them:
A tangible world and the pride of life.
The urban seagulls drift on the sky
Like words upon silence; and needles of light
Striking the water, flash as they enter.

One dark November we lost a man
Who was like this day.

POSTSCRIPT

Consistently his courage fought
Contempt of colour, creed or race.
The single faith his youth had brought
Was written on his face.

What better plan could meet his task
Than pick the wisest in the State
To solve the questions he might ask,
But now it is too late.

As politicians rise to play
The popularity they seek,
When eloquence has won the day,
Let the dead profile speak.

THAT DYING

As often as not, on fair days, there is time
for words to flex their muscles, to strut like peacocks,
discovering what to say in the act of saying—
the music of meaning emerging from the sound
of the words playing.

Every now and again, however, the glass breaks,
the alarm shrills, the women hide their faces.
It is then that words jump to their feet and rush,
like white-faced stretcher-bearers,
tight-lipped, tense, to the unspeakable scene.
They grab air, water, syllables, anything handy.
There is blood. No nonsense. No adjectives. No time.

O that these words might have been
a tourniquet of a kind, to keep
that incredible life from spattering away,
instead of as now, a dirge, a bell
tolling, a stutter, a sigh, silence.

There is nothing now for these words to do
but walk away aimlessly, mute, like mourners.

APPENDIX

From the Address of President John F. Kennedy at the Dedication of the Robert Frost Library, Amherst College, October 26, 1963

In America our heroes have customarily run to men of large accomplishments. But today this college and country honor a man whose contribution was not to our size, but to our spirit; not to our political beliefs, but to our insight; not to our self-esteem, but to our self-comprehension.

In honoring Robert Frost we therefore can pay honor to the deeper sources of our national strength. That strength takes many forms, and the most obvious forms are not always the most significant.

The men who create power make an indispensable contribution to the nation's greatness. But the men who question power make a contribution just as indispensable, especially when that questioning is disinterested.

For they determine whether we use power or power uses us. Our national strength matters; but the spirit which informs and controls our strength matters just as much. This was the special significance of Robert Frost.

He brought an unsparing instinct for reality to bear on the platitudes and pieties of society. His sense of the human tragedy fortified him against self-deception and easy consolation.

"I have been," he wrote, "one acquainted with the night."

And because he knew the midnight as well as the high noon, because he understood the ordeal as well as the triumph of the human spirit, he gave his age strength with which to overcome despair.

At bottom he held a deep faith in the spirit of man. And it's hardly an accident that Robert Frost coupled poetry and power. For he saw poetry as the means of saving power from itself.

When power leads man toward arrogance, poetry reminds him of his limitations. When power narrows the areas of man's concern, poetry reminds him of the richness and diversity of his existence. When power corrupts, poetry cleanses.

For art establishes the basic human truths which must serve as the touchstones of our judgment. The artist, however faithful to his personal vision of reality, becomes the last champion of the individual mind and sensibility against an intrusive society and an officious state.

The great artist is thus a solitary figure. He has, as Frost said, "a lover's quarrel with the world." In pursuing his perceptions of reality, he must often sail against the currents of his time. This is not a popular role.

If Robert Frost was much honored during his lifetime, it was because a good many preferred to ignore his darker truths.

Yet in retrospect we see how the artist's fidelity has strengthened the fiber of our national life. If sometimes our great artists have been the most critical of our society, it is because their sensitivity and their concern for justice, which must motivate any true artist, makes them aware that our nation falls short of its highest potential.

I see little of more importance to the future of our country and our civilization than full recognition of the place of the artist. If art is to nourish the roots of our culture, society must set the artist free to follow his vision wherever it takes him.

We must never forget that art is not a form of propaganda; it is a form of truth. And as Mr. [Archibald] MacLeish once remarked of poets, "There is nothing worse for our trade than to be in style."

In free society, art is not a weapon, and it does not belong to the sphere of polemics and ideology. Artists are not engineers of the soul.

It may be different elsewhere. But democratic society—in it—the highest duty of the writer, the composer, the artist is to remain true to himself and to let the chips fall where they may.

In serving his vision of the truth, the artist best serves his nation. And the nation which disdains the mission of art invites the fate of Robert Frost's hired man—the fate of having nothing to look backward to with pride and nothing to look forward to with hope.

I look forward to a great future for America—a future in which our country will match its military strength with our moral restraint, its wealth with our wisdom, its power with our purpose.

I look forward to an America which will not be afraid of grace and beauty, which will protect the beauty of our natural environment, which will preserve the great old American houses and squares and parks of our national past and which will build handsome and balanced cities for our future.

I look forward to an America which will reward achievement in the arts as we reward achievement in business or statecraft.

I look forward to an America which will steadily raise the standards of artistic accomplishment and which will steadily enlarge cultural opportunities for all of our citizens.

And I look forward to an America which commands respect throughout the world, not only for its strength, but for its civilization as well.

And I look forward to a world which will be safe not only for democracy and diversity but also for personal distinction.

Robert Frost was often skeptical about projects for human improvement. Yet I do not think he would disdain this hope.

NOTES ON THE POETS

A. R. AMMONS has published poetry in *The Hudson Review*, *Poetry*, *Choice*, *The Literary Review*, *Partisan Review*, *The Carleton Miscellany*, and other periodicals. His books of verse are *Ommateum* (Dorrance & Co., 1955) and *Expressions of Sea Level* (Ohio State University Press, 1964). In 1963, he was poetry editor of *The Nation*.

ALAN ANSEN's poetry has appeared in *Partisan Review*, *The Hudson Review*, *Hasty Papers*, and *Locus Solus*. His books are *The Old Religion* (Tibor de Nagy Gallery, 1959) and *Disorderly Houses* (Wesleyan University Press, 1961). Two other books of verse, *Field Report* (1963) and *Believe and Tremble* (1963), were printed in Athens in limited editions.

W. H. AUDEN is the author of numerous volumes of poems, plays, and essays. His *Collected Poetry* was published by Random House in 1945. He was awarded the Bollingen Prize for poetry in 1953 and a Pulitzer Prize for his book of verse, *The Age of Anxiety*, in 1948. Among his recent books are *Collected Shorter Poems 1930–1944* (1950), *Nones* (1951), *The Shield of Achilles* (1955), *Times Three* (1960), and a prose collection, *"The Dyer's Hand" and Other Essays* (1962). "Elegy for J. F. K." has been set to music by Igor Stravinsky.

RICHARD BARKER has published poetry in *Genesis West*, *El Corno Emplumado*, *Judson Review*, *Beatitude*, *Beatitude East*, and *Seventh Street*.

CAROL BERGÉ's poetry has appeared in *The Nation*, *Poetry*, *Fluxus*, *Origin*, *Judson Review*, and other American magazines, as well as in periodicals in England, Canada, Mexico, and Finland. Her other publications include *The Vancouver Report* (Vector Press, 1964) and contributions to *Four Young Lady Poets* (Totem/Corinth, 1963) and *Erotic Poetry* (Random House, 1963).

JOHN BERRYMAN is the author of *Poems* (New Directions, 1942), *The Dispossessed* (William Sloan Associates, 1948), *Homage to Mistress Bradstreet* (Farrar, Straus, & Cudahy, 1956), *77 Dream Songs* (Farrar, Straus, & Co., 1964), and a critical study, *Stephen Crane* (William Sloane Associates, 1950).

141

Notes on the Poets

PHILIP BOOTH has published verse in *The Atlantic Monthly, Harper's Magazine, The Nation, The New Republic, Poetry, Partisan Review, The Sewanee Review, The Paris Review,* and many other periodicals. He was awarded *Poetry's* Bess Hokin Prize in 1955, the Academy of American Poets Lamont Prize in 1956, and Guggenheim Fellowships for 1958–1959 and 1965. His books are *Letter from a Distant Land* (1957) and *The Islanders* (1961), both published by Viking. He is Associate Professor of English at Syracuse University.

GWENDOLYN BROOK's work has appeared in many American magazines. She has received a Pulitzer Prize, two Guggenheim Fellowships, the American Academy of Arts and Letters Award, and many other honors and prizes for her poetry. Among her books are *A Street in Bronzeville* (Harper & Brothers, 1945), *Annie Allen* (Harper & Brothers, 1949), *The Bean Eaters* (Harper & Brothers, 1960), and *Selected Poems* (Harper and Row, 1963).

GRAY BURR's poems have been published in *The New Yorker, Poetry, The Massachusetts Review, The Beloit Poetry Journal, New World Writing, Accent,* and *Chimera.*

WILLIAM BUTLER has published verse in *Harper's Magazine* and *Poetry Review* (London). His short stories have appeared in *Discovery, The Paris Review, Harper's Bazaar,* and *The London Magazine.* His novels, *The Experiment* (1961), *The Butterfly Revolution* (1962), *The House at Akiya* (1963), *Mr. Three* (1964; dedicated to the memory of President Kennedy), and *The Ring in Meiji* (to appear in 1965), are published by Peter Owen, Ltd. (London).

ROBERT M. CHUTE's poetry has appeared in *Bitterroot, Motive, Nimrod, South and West, Stolen Paper Review, Epos, American Weave, The Fiddlehead,* and in *Plowshare,* a journal he and his wife edit and publish in Maine. He is Chairman of the Division of Biology, Geology, and Mathematics at Bates College.

GREGORY CORSO's work has been widely published in the United States and abroad. His books are *Vestal Lady on Brattle* (Brukenfeld, 1955), *Gasoline* (City Lights, 1958), *Bomb* (a broadside; City Lights, 1959), *Happy Birthday of Death* (New Directions, 1960), and *Long Live Man* (New Directions, 1962). He won the Longview Award for his poem, "Marriage," in 1959.

GEORGE CUOMO has published poetry in *Saturday Review, The Nation, The Massachusetts Review, The Literary Review,*

142

Notes on the Poets

Voices, The Carolina Quarterly, and other magazines. His novels, *Jack Be Nimble* (1963) and *Bright Day, Dark Runner* (1964), were published by Doubleday. He is Associate Professor of English at the University of Victoria, Canada.

GEORGE DEKKER is Lecturer in Literature at the University of Essex, England. His verse has appeared in *Prospect* and in *Spectrum.* He is the author of *Sailing after Knowledge: The Cantos of Ezra Pound* (Routledge & Kegan Paul, 1963).

RICHARD EBERHART's recent books include *Undercliff: Poems 1946–1953* (1953) and *Great Praises* (1957), both published by Oxford University Press in New York and Chatto and Windus in London. His *Collected Poems* appeared in 1960, and his *Collected Verse Plays* in 1962. *The Quarry* (1964) is his latest book of poems. He was Consultant in Poetry at the Library of Congress for 1959–1961, and in 1959 he was appointed by President Eisenhower to the Advisory Committee on the Arts for the National Cultural Center in Washington, D.C. In 1963, he was named Honorary Consultant in American Letters for 1963–1966 by the Library of Congress. Since 1956, he has been Professor of English and Poet in Residence at Dartmouth College.

CHANA FAERSTEIN is a graduate student at Brandeis University specializing in Near Eastern and Judaic Studies. Her poetry, critical articles, and verse translations have appeared in numerous periodicals.

G. S. FRASER's verse has been published in *New Statesman, The Times Literary Supplement, The New York Review of Books, Poetry* (London), and *Poetry* (Chicago). His books of poetry are *The Fatal Landscape* (1942), *Home Town Elegy* (1944), and *The Traveller Has Regrets* (1947), all published by Editions Poetry London, the last in combination with Harvill Press. His other books are *Vision and Rhetoric* (Faber and Faber, 1959) and *The Modern Writer and His World* (Penguin Books, 1964). He is Visiting Professor of English at the University of Rochester.

RICHARD FROST has published poems in *Poetry, The Sewanee Review, Harper's Magazine, Prairie Schooner, The Carleton Miscellany, The Literary Review, Southwest Review,* and other magazines.

ROBERT FROST (1874–1963) wrote "For John F. Kennedy His Inauguration" in response to Mr. Kennedy's invitation to participate in the inauguration ceremonies. At the inauguration,

Notes on the Poets

Frost read "The Gift Outright." *Complete Poems of Robert Frost* was published by Henry Holt and Company in 1949. His last book of poems, *In the Clearing*, appeared in 1962.

R O Y F U L L E R has published a number of books of verse, the most recent of which is his *Collected Poems* (Deutsch, 1962), and several novels, the latest of which is *The Perfect Fool* (Deutsch, 1963).

D O R O T H Y G I L B E R T ' S poetry has appeared in *The New Yorker*. She won the Morrison Poetry Prize at Cornell University in 1957.

A L L E N G I N S B E R G ' S books of poetry are *"Howl" and Other Poems* (City Lights, 1956), *"Kaddish" and Other Poems* (City Lights, 1960), *Empty Mirror: Early Poems* (Totem/Corinth, 1961), *Reality Sandwiches* (City Lights, 1963), and, in collaboration with William Burroughs, *Yage Letters* (City Lights, 1964).

M I C H A E L G O L D M A N has published poetry in *The New Yorker, Poetry, The Atlantic Monthly, The Kenyon Review, The Yale Review, The Minnesota Review, The Virginia Quarterly Review*, and *The Massachusetts Review*. Macmillan is to publish his first volume of verse in 1965.

P A U L G O O D M A N has published poetry in *The Nation, Poetry, The Kenyon Review, Partisan Review*, and other periodicals. His recent books are *The Lordly Hudson* and *Making Do*, both published by Macmillan in 1963. He is the author of *The Empire City* (Bobbs-Merrill, 1959) and *Growing Up Absurd* (Random House, 1960). He is a Fellow of the Institute for Policy Studies and has won a National Institute of Arts and Letters Award.

R A L P H G O R D O N ' S poetry has been published in *The Yale Review, The Atlantic Monthly, Commentary, The American Poet*, and other magazines. He is Professor of English at The City College of New York.

B A R B A R A G U E S T ' S poetry has appeared in *Evergreen Review, Partisan Review, Poetry, Locus Solus, Art and Literature, Noonday Review, Yugen, "C" Magazine*, and other periodicals. Her books are *Location of Things* (Tibor de Nagy Gallery, 1960), *Poems* (Doubleday, 1962), and *Robert Goodnough* (Éditions de Poche, 1963). She has held a Yaddo Fellowship and was the recipient of a Longview Foundation Award for her poetry.

D O N A L D H A L L ' S poems have appeared in *The Nation, New Statesman, Encounter, Poetry*, and in numerous other periodicals.

144

His books of verse are *Exiles and Marriages* (1955), *The Dark Houses* (1958), and *A Roof of Tiger Lilies* (1964), all published by Viking. He has held a Guggenheim Fellowship and was elected to the Society of Fellows at Harvard.

R O B E R T   H A Z E L has published poetry in *New Directions 12* and *14*, *Poetry*, *The Minnesota Review*, *Prairie Schooner*, *The Nation*, and *Choice*. His books are *Poems 1951–61* (Morehead Press, Kentucky, 1961) and two novels, *The Lost Year* (1953) and *A Field Full of People* (1954), both published by World Publishing Company. He was Saxon Memorial Fellow in Fiction in 1955. He is Professor of English at New York University.

G E O R G E   H I T C H C O C K has published poetry in *The Massachusetts Review*, *The Paris Review*, *The Minnesota Review*, *Prairie Schooner*, *San Francisco Review*, *The Sixties*, *Choice*, and many other reviews. His books are *Poems and Prints* (Amber House, 1962) and *Tactics of Survival* (Bindweed Press, 1964).

R O B E R T   H O L L A N D E R ' S poetry has appeared in *The Kenyon Review*, *The Georgia Review*, *The Second Coming Magazine*, and *Columbia University Forum*. His translation of André Malraux's *The Temptation of the West* was published by Vintage in 1961. He edited *A Poetry Reader* (American Book Company, 1963).

A N S E L M   H O L L O has published poetry in periodicals in the United States, England, and Mexico. He is the author of *Texts & Finnpoems* (Migrant Press, 1960), *loverman* (the dead language press, 1963), *history* (Matrix Press, 1964), and *The Man in the Treetop Hat* (Fantasy Press: Oxford, 1964). He is Program Assistant for the British Broadcasting System's European Services.

B A R B A R A   H O W E S's poetry has appeared in *The New Yorker*, *Harper's Bazaar*, *Partisan Review*, *Encounter*, *Poetry*, *The Sewanee Review*, *The Nation*, *The New Republic*, and many other periodicals. Her books of poetry are *The Undersea Farmer* (The Banyan Press, 1948), *In the Cold Country* (Bonacio & Saul, with Grove Press, 1954), and *Light and Dark* (Wesleyan University Press, 1959). She was awarded a Guggenheim Fellowship in 1955, the Brandeis University Creative Arts Poetry Grant for 1958, and prizes from *Poetry* in 1949 and 1959.

R I C H A R D   F.   H U G O has published poetry in *Accent*, *Contact*, *Poetry*, *Poetry Northwest*, *The Yale Review*, *The Massachusetts Review*, *The Paris Review*, *Transatlantic Review*, *Botteghe Oscure*, and many other reviews. He is the author of *A Run of Jacks* (University of Minnesota Press, 1961). A new book of his poems, *Death of the Kapowsin Tavern*, will be published by Harcourt, Brace & World in 1965.

DAVID IGNATOW's poetry has been published in many magazines, including *Poetry*, *The Yale Review*, *The Nation*, *Commentary*, *Saturday Review*, *The Sixties*, and *The Carleton Miscellany*. He is the author of *Poems* (Decker Press, 1948), *The Gentle Weight Lifter* (Morris Gallery, 1955), *Say Pardon* (Wesleyan University Press, 1961), and *Figures of the Human* (Wesleyan University Press, 1964). He edited *The Beloit Poetry Journal's* Whitman Centennial issue in 1955 and that magazine's William Carlos Williams Memorial Chapbook in 1963. He was poetry editor of *The Nation* in 1963.

WILL INMAN's poetry has appeared in *Epos*, *The Fiddlehead*, *Mutiny*, *motive*, *Poet* (India), *Umbra*, *Image*, and other poetry magazines. He is the author of *I Am the Snakehandler* (1960), *Lamen & Psalm* (1960), *A River of Laughter* (1961), all published by the New Athenaeum Press, *Honey in Hot Blood* (Bitter Root Press, 1962), and *108 Verges unto Now* (Carlton Press, 1964).

DONALD L. JONES teaches English at the University of Nebraska. His poems have appeared in *Prairie Schooner*, *Channels*, and *Gallery*. He was awarded an Academy of American Poets Prize in 1963.

WALTER KAUFMANN has published poetry in *The American Scholar*, *Harper's Magazine*, *The Menorah Journal*, and *University*. Among his many books are *Cain and Other Poems* (Doubleday, 1962), *Goethe's Faust: A New Translation* (Doubleday, 1961), and *Twenty German Poets* (Random House, 1962). Professor of Philosophy at Princeton University, he has published numerous philosophical studies and edited *Existentialism from Dostoevsky to Sartre* (Meridian Books, 1956).

X. J. KENNEDY's poetry has been published in *The New Yorker*, *The Paris Review*, *Poetry*, *The Hudson Review*, and many other periodicals. His book of poems, *Nude Descending a Staircase*, was published by Doubleday in 1961. The same year, he was awarded the Bess Hokin Prize by *Poetry* and the Lamont Prize by the Academy of American Poets.

STANLEY KOEHLER has published poetry in *The Sewanee Review*, *The Yale Review*, *Poetry*, *The Massachusetts Review*, and

Voices. A collection of his verse, "A Winter Gardener," appeared in *A Curious Quire* (University of Massachusetts Press, 1962). He is Professor of English at the University of Massachusetts and co-editor of poetry for *The Massachusetts Review.*

MYRON LEVOY'S poems have appeared in *The Antioch Review, The Massachusetts Review, Chelsea, Mutiny, The Wormwood Review, The Midwest Quarterly, Coastlines,* and other periodicals.

AUDREY McGAFFIN has published in *The Stylus, Whetstone, Imagi, Shenandoah, Voices, The Saturday Evening Post, Talisman, Spirit, Contact, New Poems by American Poets #1* (Balantine Books, 1953) and *#2* (1957), and *Epos Anthology* (New Athenaeum Press, 1954). Her volume of verse is *The Imagined Country* (Editions Imagi, 1957).

OSCAR MANDEL has published in *The Hudson Review, The Northwest Review, The Literary Review, Prairie Schooner, Epoch, The Western Humanities Review, San Francisco Review,* and many other periodicals. He is the author of *A Definition of Tragedy* (New York University Press, 1961), *The Theatre of Don Juan* (University of Nebraska Press, 1963), and *Chi Po and the Sorcerer* (Charles E. Tuttle, 1964). He is Associate Professor of Humanities at the California Institute of Technology.

JACK MARSHALL'S poetry has appeared in *Harper's Magazine, New World Writing, Poetry, The Hudson Review, Contact, Epoch, The New Yorker, The Second Coming Magazine, The Plumed Horn, Mademoiselle, The Paris Review,* and *Between Worlds.*

JOSEPHINE MILES has published poems in *The Kenyon Review, The Nation, Poetry, The Sewanee Review, The Massachusetts Review,* and *The Carleton Miscellany.* Her books include *Lines at Intersection* (Macmillan, 1939), *Poems on Several Occasions* (New Directions, 1941), *Poems 1930–1960* (Indiana University Press, 1957), *Eras and Modes in English Poetry* (2nd ed.; University of California Press, 1964), and *Emerson* (University of Minnesota Press, 1964). She won the Poetry Society of America's Shelley Memorial Award (1935), a Guggenheim Fellowship (1948), an Institute of Arts and Letters Award (1957), and an American Council of Learned Societies Fellowship (1964–1965). She is Professor of English at the University of California at Berkeley.

MARJORIE MIR is Children's Librarian at the New York

Notes on the Poets

Public Library. "Four Days in November" is the first of her poems to be published.

H o w a r d M o s s ' s poems have appeared in *The New Yorker, Partisan Review, The Kenyon Review, The Paris Review, The Nation, The New Republic, Harper's Magazine, Botteghe Oscure*, and many other periodicals. He is the author of *The Wound and the Weather* (Reynal and Hitchcock, 1946), *The Toy Fair* (Scribner's, 1954), *A Swimmer in the Air* (Scribner's, 1957), *Keats* (Dell, 1959), *A Winter Come, A Summer Gone* (Scribner's, 1960), and *The Magic Lantern of Marcel Proust* (Macmillan, 1962). He is Poetry Editor of *The New Yorker*.

H. L. M o u n t z o u r e s published an *Atlantic* "First" short story in the Fall of 1964.

N e i l M y e r s has published poems in *Chelsea, The Massachusetts Review, The Minnesota Review, Targets, Sparrow, Quartet, Audience, Audit, South and West*, and *The New York Times*. He was one of the founding editors of *The Minnesota Review*. He is Assistant Professor of English at Purdue University.

R i c h a r d O ' C o n n e l l has published poems in *The Paris Review, Evergreen Review, Botteghe Oscure, The Texas Quarterly*, and many other periodicals. He is the author of *From an Interior Silence* (Contemporary Poetry, 1961), *Cries of Flesh and Stone* (Atlantis Editions, Philadelphia, 1962), and *New Poems and Translations* (Atlantis Editions, Pamplona, 1963). He has twice been Fulbright Lecturer in American Literature: in Rio de Janeiro, Brazil (1960), and in Pamplona, Spain (1962–1963). He is Assistant Professor of English at Temple University.

A n t h o n y O s t r o f f has published poems and stories in many magazines, among which are *Accent, Epoch, Perspective, The Atlantic Monthly, Harper's Magazine, Poetry, Poetry London–New York, Saturday Review, The Chicago Review, Genesis West, The Kenyon Review*, and *The Paris Review*. He is the author of *Imperatives* (Harcourt, Brace & World, 1962) and the editor of *The Contemporary Poet as Artist and Critic* (Little, Brown & Co., 1964). He has been a Fulbright Fellow (France, 1950), a Fellow of the Yaddo Foundation (1954 and 1957), a Robert Frost Fellow (1958), and a Fellow of the University of California Institute for the Creative Arts (1964). He is Associate Professor at the University of California at Berkeley.

C y n t h i a O z i c k has published in *Commentary, Midstream,*

148

Epoch, Prairie Schooner, The Literary Review, New Mexico Quarterly, The Virginia Quarterly Review, Mutiny, Chelsea, San Francisco Review, The Noble Savage, and many other magazines. Her long novel, *Trust,* is to be published by McGraw-Hill.

E D W A R D   P O L S, Chairman of the Department of Philosophy at Bowdoin College, is, like the late President Kennedy, a member of the Class of 1940 at Harvard. He is the author of *The Recognition of Reason* (Southern Illinois University Press, 1963).

D A V I D   R A Y has published poems in *Accent, The Paris Review, The Nation, The New Republic, Quarterly Review of Literature, Poetry, Poetry Northwest,* and many other periodicals. He is the author of a volume of poems, *X-Rays* (Cornell University Press, 1964). He edited *The Chicago Review Anthology* (University of Chicago Press, 1959) and *Poems at the Hungarian Revolution* (Cornell University Press, 1964). In 1958, he won *The New Republic*'s Young Writers Award. He is Assistant Professor of Literature and Humanities at Reed College.

A L A S T A I R   R E I D has published poems in *The New Yorker, Encounter, Poetry,* and many other magazines. He is the author of *Ounce Dice Trice* (1958), *Oddments Inklings Omens Moments* (1960), and *Passwords* (1963), all published by Atlantic-Little, Brown & Co. He was awarded Guggenheim Fellowships in 1955 and 1956.

R A Y M O N D   R O S E L I E P is a Roman Catholic priest whose poems have appeared in *Poetry, The Nation, Modern Age, Chicago Review, The Colorado Quarterly, The Massachusetts Review, Prairie Schooner, Shenandoah,* and many other magazines. He is the author of *The Linen Bands* (The Newman Press, 1961) and *The Small Rain* (The Newman Press, 1961). He is Associate Professor of English at Loras College and poetry editor of *Sponsa Regis.*

J E R O M E   G.   R O T H E N B E R G teaches Economics at Northwestern University. He is the author of *The Measurement of Social Welfare* (Prentice-Hall, 1961) and *Economic Evaluation of Urban Renewal* (The Brookings Institution, 1964). His poems have appeared in *Chicago Review, Commentary,* and *The Columbia Review.*

H A R V E Y   S H A P I R O has published poetry in *Quarterly Review of Literature, Poetry, Commentary, Midstream, Chelsea, Epoch, The Nation, The Beloit Poetry Journal,* and *Saturday Review.* His books of verse are *The Eye* (Alan Swallow, 1953), *The Book and*

Notes on the Poets

Other Poems (The Cummington Press, 1955), and *Mountain, Fire, Thornbush* (Alan Swallow, 1961).

ROBIN SKELTON has published poetry in *The Listener, The New Statesman, The London Magazine, The Observer, Poetry, Poetry Northwest, The Times Literary Supplement, The Massachusetts Review,* and many other periodicals. His books of verse include *Third Day Lucky* (1958), *Begging the Dialect* (1960), and *The Dark Window* (1962), all published by Oxford University Press. He edited *Six Irish Poets* (Oxford University Press, 1962) and J. M. Synge's *Collected Poems* (Oxford University Press, 1964). He is Associate Professor of English at the University of Victoria, Canada.

MARVIN SOLOMON has published poems in *Poetry, The New Yorker, Imagi, The Hudson Review, The Paris Review, New Mexico Quarterly, Shenandoah, The Massachusetts Review, The Literary Review,* and *Prairie Schooner.* He is the author of *First Poems* (Editions Imagi, 1952), *The Royal Tiger's Face* (Contemporary Poetry, 1960), and *A View from Africa* (Contemporary Poetry, 1962).

BARRY SPACKS has published poetry in *The American Scholar, The Atlantic Monthly, Chicago Review, The Antioch Review, Poetry, The Yale Review, Mademoiselle, The Noble Savage, Shenandoah, Interim, The Carleton Miscellany, The Massachusetts Review,* and other magazines. He was a Fulbright Fellow to England (1956–1957) and is now Assistant Professor of Humanities at the Massachusetts Institute of Technology.

ADRIEN STOUTENBURG has published poems in *The New Yorker, The Nation, The Yale Review, San Francisco Review, Epoch, Commonweal,* and many other magazines. Her volumes of verse include *Heroes Advise Us* (Scribner's, 1964) and a book of poems for children, *The Things That Are* (Reilly & Lee, 1964). She won the Edwin Markham Award and the Michael Sloane Award, both given by the Poetry Society of America, in 1962.

DABNEY STUART has published in *Poetry, The Antioch Review, Southern Poetry Today, Epos, Impetus, Best Articles and Stories of 1961, The William and Mary Review, The Lyric, The Southwest Review,* and *The Southern Poetry Review.* He was a Woodrow Wilson Fellow at Harvard (1961). He teaches English at the College of William and Mary.

150

Notes on the Poets

ROBERT SWARD has published poetry in *The Nation, Poetry, The Antioch Review, The Massachusetts Review,* and other periodicals. He is the author of *"Uncle Dog" and Other Poems* (Putnam & Co., Ltd., 1962) and *"Kissing the Dancer" and Other Poems* (Cornell University Press, 1964). He was awarded a Fulbright Fellowship (England, 1960–1961) and a Guggenheim Fellowship (1964–1965). He teaches English at Cornell University.

MAY SWENSON has published poems in *The Nation, Saturday Review, The New Yorker, Harper's Magazine, Poetry, The Carleton Miscellany,* and many other periodicals. She is the author of *"Another Animal: Poems," Poets of Today I* (Scribner's, 1954), *A Cage of Spines* (Rinehart & Co., 1958), and *To Mix with Time, New and Selected Poems* (Scribner's, 1963). She has been awarded a Guggenheim Fellowship, a National Institute of Arts and Letters Award, a Robert Frost Fellowship, an Amy Lowell Traveling Scholarship, and a Ford Foundation Poet-Theater grant.

JOHN TAGLIABUE has published poems in *Poetry, Saturday Review, Chicago Review, The Virginia Quarterly Review, Orient/ West, Prairie Schooner,* and many other periodicals. He is the author of *Poems* (Harper and Brothers, 1959). He was Fulbright Lecturer in American Literature in Italy (1950–1952) and in Japan (1958–1960) and now teaches at Bates College in Maine.

LORENZO THOMAS has published poetry in *The Art Journal, The Rivoli Review, Umbra, The Wagner Literary Review,* and other periodicals. In 1963, he won the John Golden Prize at Queens College.

ROBERT G. TUCKER has published poems in *The Massachusetts Review, The Minister's Quarterly, Monument,* and other periodicals. A collection of his poems, "A Way of Looking," appeared in *A Curious Quire* (University of Massachusetts Press, 1962). He is Assistant Professor of English at the University of Massachusetts.

LEWIS TURCO has published poems in *The Kenyon Review, The Antioch Review, The Sewanee Review, Poetry, The American Scholar,* and other periodicals. He is the author of *First Poems* (Golden Quill Press, 1960) and *The Sketches* (American Weave Press, 1962). In 1960, he won an Academy of American Poets Prize. He is the founder and former director of the Cleveland Poetry Center.

151

Notes on the Poets

FLORENCE VICTOR has published poems in *The Beloit Poetry Journal, The Critic, Commentary, The Fiddlehead, Poetry, Poetry Northwest, The Second Coming Magazine, The Transatlantic Review,* and *The Wormwood Review.* In 1958, she won the John Golden Award at Queens College.

VERNON WATKINS has published in many periodicals in the United States and Great Britain. He is the author of *"Ballad of the Mari Lwyd" and Other Poems* (1941), *Selected Poems* (1948), *The Death Bell* (1954), *Cypress and Acacia* (1959), and *Affinities* (1962), all published by New Directions. He edited Dylan Thomas' *Letters to Vernon Watkins* (New Directions, 1959). He was a Fellow of the Royal Society of Literature (1951) and was awarded The Levinson Prize for Poetry (1955) and The Guinness Prize for Poetry (1957).

ROBERT WATSON has published poetry in *The American Scholar, Poetry, The Paris Review, The Transatlantic Review,* and many other periodicals. He is the author of *"A Paper Horse" and Other Poems* (Atheneum, 1962). He is Professor of English at the University of North Carolina at Greensboro.

JAMES L. WEIL has published poems in *The American Weave, Coffin, Combustion, Hawk and Whippoorwill, Gallows, The Goliards, Hearse, Micromegus, Penny Poems from Amarillo,* and other magazines. His books of verse are *Quarrel with the Rose* (1958), *A Fool Turns Clockwise* (1960), and *Sorrow's Spy* (1961), all published by The American Weave Press, and *The Oboe Player* (Golden Quill Press, 1961). In 1958, he won the American Weave Chapbook Award. He is Editor and Publisher of The Elizabeth Press.

THOMAS WHITBREAD'S poetry has appeared in *Harper's Magazine, The Atlantic, The Carleton Miscellany, The Kenyon Review, The Paris Review, The Texas Observer, Triad, The Virginia Quarterly Review,* and many other publications. His book of poems, *Four Infinitives,* was published by Harper & Row in 1964.

REED WHITTEMORE is Consultant in Poetry at the Library of Congress for 1964–1965. He is Professor of English at Carleton College and Editor of *The Carleton Miscellany.* His poems have appeared in *Poetry, The New Republic, The Sewanee Review,* and many other periodicals. He is the author of *Heroes and Heroines* (Reynal and Hitchcock, 1947), *An American Takes a Walk* (University of Minnesota Press, 1956), *The Self-Made Man* (Macmillan, 1959), *The Boy from Iowa* (Macmillan, 1962), and *The Fascination of the Abomination* (Macmillan, 1963).

JONATHAN WILLIAMS is Publisher of Jargon Books and President of The Nantahala Foundation. His poems have appeared in *Evergreen Review, Vogue, Black Mountain Review, Origin, Kulchur*, and other periodicals. He is the author of *The Empire Finals at Verona* (Jargon Books, 1959), *In England's Green &* (Auerhahn Press, 1962), *Lullabies Twisters Gibbers Drags* (Jargon Books, 1963), *Lines about Hills above Lakes* (Roman Books, 1964) and *Blues & Roots/Rue & Bluets* (Folkways, 1964). He was awarded a Guggenheim Fellowship for 1957–1958, and in 1960 he received a Longview Foundation Grant.

CHARLES WRIGHT has published poems in *The Carleton Miscellany, The Massachusetts Review, Poetry Northwest, The North American Review, Chelsea*, and *The Oberlin Quarterly*. He won an Academy of American Poets Prize at the University of Iowa (1962) and a Fulbright Fellowship to Italy (1963–1965).

GEORGE T. WRIGHT, Associate Professor of English at the University of Tennessee, has published poetry in *The New Yorker, The Berkeley Review, East and West, Number*, and other periodicals. He is the author of *The Poet in the Poem: The Personae of Eliot, Yeats, and Pound* (University of California Press, 1960). He is Fulbright Lecturer in American Literature at the University of Aix-Marseille, France (1964–1965).

RUTH LANDSHOFF YORCK has published poems in *Tomorrow, The Massachusetts Review, The Tiger's Eye, Folder, Nul, Salon 13, Du, Frankfurter Hefte, Jardin des Modes, Quadrigue, The Transatlantic Review, The London Magazine*, and many other periodicals.

LOUIS ZUKOFSKY has published poetry in *Botteghe Oscure, Black Mountain Review, Contact, Criterion, Dial, Exile, Hound and Horn, Poetry, Origin, The Paris Review*, and many other periodicals. His books include *Some Time* (Jargon Books, 1956), *"A" 1-12* (Origin Press, 1959), and *Bottom: on Shakespeare* (University of Texas Press, 1963). He was Poet in Residence at San Francisco State College in 1958 and won The Longview Award in 1961.

ACKNOWLEDGMENTS

Grateful acknowledgment is here made for permission to reprint poems:

"Footnote to Lord Acton," by Cynthia Ozick, is reprinted by permission of Miss Ozick and *The Virginia Quarterly Review.*

"No Retreat" is reprinted with permission of The Macmillan Company from *The Fascination of the Abomination,* by Reed Whittemore, copyright 1961 by Reed Whittemore.

"Mr. Kennedy Proposes to Pacify the Caribbeans," by George Hitchcock, is reprinted by permission of *Burning Water.*

"Long Lines," by Paul Goodman, is reprinted by permission of Mr. Goodman and *The New York Review of Books.*

"November 22, 1963," by Lewis Turco (copyright 1964, The Modern Poetry Association), was first published in the November, 1964, issue of *Poetry* and is reprinted here by permission of Mr. Turco and the editor of *Poetry.*

"In Identity," by Josephine Miles, is reprinted by permission of *Oyez.*

"At the Brooklyn Docks," by Dorothy Gilbert, © 1964 The New Yorker Magazine, Inc.

"Spider Head," by Donald Hall (copyright 1964, The Modern Poetry Association), was first published in the May, 1964, issue of *Poetry* and is reprinted here by permission of Mr. Hall and the editor of *Poetry.*

"Instead of an Elegy," by G. S. Fraser, is reprinted here by permission of Mr. Fraser, *The New York Review of Books,* and *The Times Literary Supplement.*

"Elegy for the New Year," copyright © 1964 by Jack Marshall.

"National Cold Storage Company," by Harvey Shapiro, is reprinted by permission of Mr. Shapiro and *Quarterly Review of Literature.*

"Lines for a President," by Robert Watson, is reprinted by permission of *The American Scholar.*

"A Kind of Libation," by James L. Weil, is reprinted by permission of *The Goliards.*

"For John Kennedy, Jr.," by Raymond Roseliep, is reprinted by permission of *Charlatan.*

"Elegy for J. F. K.," copyright © 1964 by W. H. Auden.

"That Dying," by Alastair Reid, © 1964 The New Yorker Magazine, Inc.